CRACKING THE GLASS DARKLY

THE ANCIENT PATH TO LASTING HAPPINESS

CRACKING THE GLASS DARKLY

THE ANCIENT PATH TO LASTING HAPPINESS

Robert Egby

Author of the award-winning books:

The Quest of the Radical Spiritualist
INSIGHTS: The Healing Paths of the Radical Spiritualist

Three Mile Point Publishing
Chaumont, NY

First published 2008

Revised and updated edition published: April 2011
Three Mile Point Publishing
Chaumont, NY

ISBN: 978-0-9832404-1-9
Library of Congress Control Number: 2011922184

Printed in the United States of America

This book is gratefully dedicated to all the Students who came to my classes and workshops and helped me to learn.

CONTENTS

INTRODUCTION
HOW DID WE GET SO SCREWED UP?

I wish someone had told me a whole bunch of years ago that I am a lovable, intricate, intelligent, creative, beautiful human being – all the things I later learned from a unique spiritual philosopher named Paul Solomon who lived in Edgar Cayce's hometown, Virginia Beach.

I wish someone had taught me when the WWII bombs were falling around that high school at Maidenhead, 26 miles west of London, that the negative, hurtful ego I was developing was not the true me, that there was a way of dissolving it, and being able to live with the true self, the lovable self, the self that is part of the Creator, Infinite Intelligence. I often wonder if Mr. Clough, the best teacher I ever had, who inspired me to write and travel, really ever knew the existence of a true self. I think he did.

He once mentioned the ancient Aryans of India, but he never told us about how they possessed a special knowledge, a special mystical consciousness, and some had migrated to Persia and developed their own Cosmic Consciousness, their own Awareness that ousts the dreaded ego from the mind. They became known as the Sufis, the wool gatherers, a mystical sect of Islam.

And even if the teachers at Gordon Road Secondary School had known about the Sufis, and how the Russian philosopher George Ivanovitch Gurdjieff had spent 15 years trekking and learning in desert homes and temples studying the human mind, body and spirit, post-war British society would not have allowed them to share such radical thinking with teenage students. At the Chateau de

Prieure at Fontainebleau-Avon Gurdjieff created a teaching center which attracted students from many parts of the world. The principal teaching was focused on waking his students from a life of daydreams and subjective biases. He taught students to live, understand and enjoy the ecstasy of living in the here and now.

When in the mid-1950s I hung out in Jerusalem and did a bunch of stories on the battles between Arabs and Jews. At the Hadassah University I discussed with scientists the meanings of the Dead Sea Scrolls, and had many lunches with the seemingly worldly Father Roc and the nuns at the Convent of the Sisters of Zion yet no one ever mention the afterlife. Did Father Roc who was a veritable mine of information on the Church of the Holy Sepulchre understand the true meaning of the Easter Sunday Resurrection, and if so, why did he not share it with me?

And later, when I explored the highways and byways of metaphysics and learned all about intuition, clairvoyance, clairaudience and clairsentience – the faculty of being psychic – it dawned on me that back in the last days (1955-1960) of the British island colony of Cyprus in the eastern Mediterranean when I was a journalist and news photographer covering the Greek Cypriots' violent struggle for independence, that "something" or "someone" was guiding me to be in the right place for a story.

Britain's Daily Telegraph, which published many of my news photos, actually pondered in print, why I should be at the scene of so many incidents. No one ever suggested I might be intuitive. No one ever told me about being psychic. Not even the Hindu Yogi who came into the Cyprus Mail offices one day and told me: "You will go to the far side of the Americas – you will come back through the darkness into the light and you will know and understand the meaning of the One Self – that which is the true self within you."

Later, I laughed, and told some reporters over drinks that night in Antonakis Bar in the old city of Nicosia how "bloody stupid" the words from the Yogi were. No one ever told me about my mechanical mind, the shallow, totally ignorant Ego talking. I never dreamt for one moment that I would see the day when the old man's prediction came true. But it did.

Many years after Cyprus, when I was living in Vancouver, British Columbia, I discovered that there is life after death, that all does not end in dust on Boot Hill, and that it is possible, in fact dead easy to talk to loved ones who have passed on into another world – the Astral Planes of the Yogis and the Spirit World of the Spiritualists.

Patrick Young, the British medium and teacher at the Vancouver Psychic Society told us in closed-circle: "If you want to be a good medium, you have to get yourself out of the way." When someone asked him to explain, he laughed, and said: "You need to kill the Ego. It's your False Self. Depending on its force it will taint your work as a medium – messages will be tainted with your own inclinations, limitations and biases."

Then he added: "Even if you don't decide to embark on mediumship, killing the Ego will allow you to find your One Self – your True Self." I suddenly recalled the words of the Indian Yogi in far off Nicosia. "You will come through the darkness into the light."

For some years prior to finding out about enlightenment, higher awareness and metaphysics, I had suffered through what St. John of the Cross aptly described as the "Dark Night of the Soul." In mysticism, this is when a person undergoes a major change in his or her physical, mental and spiritual life. Everything seems to fall apart – career, family, social relationships, financial standing, and health. There is suffering, bewilderment, and deep hurts and the condition may last a few months or a few years. The dark night rarely lasts more than five years.

After twenty-five years as a journalist, news photographer, broadcaster, and editor, and grossly overweight from eating fast foods, and satisfying some inner urge to smoke forty cigarettes a day which took me through long working hours, and frustrated from a lack of substantial income, I quit the media. I went into public relations where the financial rewards were better.

Outwardly I enjoyed the challenges of handling the media at Weyerhaeuser Canada, The Insurance Corporation of British Columbia, and the building of SkyTrain, the first driverless automated rapid transit in North America. The professional life looked great, but something was missing. In spite of the fact that professional life was interesting, creative and satisfying, my private life, my inner life felt stagnant, a black gaping hole.

The fast addictive life of exciting, even dangerous journalism reached out to me. But I knew I could not go back. My whole self felt wrong. The ego was eruptive. I became angry, disillusioned, jealous, excessively judgmental, fearful, bitter, confused, conceited and insecure. My relationship with family and the people I had loved crashed. My Vancouver physician Dr. Borkenhagen told me: "You're out of control. You may not last too long."

Dying? Death? The idea was foreign to my mind. I had spent thirteen years in the turbulent, war-torn Middle East photographing riots, assassinations, being attacked by a mob, rode in a helicopter that sustained machine gun fire as an accredited War Correspondent at the Suez Invasion of 1956, had friends who I didn't know were active terrorists, and unknowingly walked through an unmarked minefield in northern Lebanon – and lived. Somehow, my ego had always told me I was immortal. In my suffering I was suddenly conscious that all this was wrong...very wrong.

I started walking and eventually jogging along Vancouver's English Bay to Jericho Beach. These are meditative states which made me curious. One weekend I attended a workshop at the University of Columbia where I learned Self Hypnosis and Meditation from Dr. Lee Pulos. Although that was over thirty years ago, I can still hear his mellow tones chanting so effectively. Meditation, I found, helped me to stay balanced. During my years in Public Relations, I had spent my spare time writing four novels which turned out to be ornaments or dust-gatherers on the shelf of a Toronto literary agent.

Then one day, a little voice said: "Write a psychic novel. Find out how psychics and mediums work." Psychics were phonies, I started to think, but my mind shot back to Nicosia and the Hindu Yogi in far-off Cyprus: "You will go to the far side of the Americas – you will come back through the darkness into the light." Another part of me wanted to agree the ancient had been right. I wanted to get back into the light. I was still hesitant and leery. If the old Yogi from Cyprus had appeared before me I would have yelled: "All right, so I'm meditating and exercising my butt off. What do you want me to do now?" He wasn't there. But the little voice was there insisting I write a psychic novel.

A researcher by heart, I started reading books on metaphysics, the philosophies of Yoga, Buddhism, Judaism, Hinduism, Jainism, Taoism, and Zen. There was Upton Sinclair's Mental Radio, Joseph Weed's Wisdom of the Mystic Masters and Fodor's Psychic Encyclopedia. I started interviewing psychics and discovered that most of them didn't know how "things-psychic" worked. They knew it worked, but how...well, that was something else.

I attended night-school classes given by a Brazilian medium and discovered that simply by holding an object hidden in a brown paper bag, I had visions of what was inside – a china vase with a pink rose embossed on the outside. One day I had a psychic reading with long-time British Columbia Spiritualist, Rev. Gloria Brough. "I'm not going to read for you," she said bluntly. "Check in with Isabel Corlett at the Vancouver Psychic Society."

Isabel made me welcome and two weeks later British medium Patrick Young, a happy soul with a blond complexion, a great teacher of mediumship, but possessing a snappy temper, took me into his Friday night closed circle. It was accelerated learning. I discovered my psychic abilities quite easily – and I could sense spirits. Two years later, I started conducting weekly classes on psychic development, and I stayed there for ten years. Early in the decade I found out that although I was being psychic and performing hands-on healing, there was still something missing.

Creatively I wrote meditations and lectures for the students at the Psychic Society, made public platform presentations on psychometry, clairvoyance, astral projection, and gave hands-on healing at the weekly meetings. I still felt irritable, annoyed, angry inside. The ego no longer hurt so much, but it was still evident. I sorely missed the thrills and urgency of the journalistic life, but a voice inside insisted: "You can't go back."

One Saturday morning at a dusty, second-hand bookstore on Vancouver's Granville Street, someone standing next to me thrust a paperback into my hands. "Have you read this?" Surprised, I looked at the cover. It was by a fellow named Alan Watts and the title was intriguing: "The Book On the Taboo Against Knowing Who You Are."

My fingers flipped through the pages. I discovered an interesting paragraph by Dr. Watts. "The lowdown on life is that our normal sensation of self is a hoax or, at best, a temporary role that we are playing, or have been conned into playing..." Then he adds: "The most strongly enforced of all known taboos is the taboo against knowing who or what you really are behind the mask of your apparently separate, independent and isolated ego."

Masks? What masks? Did I really wear masks? In the days and weeks that followed I studied books by Yogi Ramacharaka, Richard M. Bucke, J. Krishnamurti and more. Stuart Wilde came to town and I listened to him and other visiting mystics. That classic book "The Lazy Man's Guide to Enlightenment" by Thaddeus Golas came into my life and I found an interesting quotation that haunted me for quite a while: "Whatever you are doing, love yourself for doing it."

That puzzled me for ages and the desire and passion to find out all about the mystery masks of Dr. Watts, and the impossible love quotation of Thaddeus Golas drove me through bookshops, meditation groups, New Age film shows, but the truth - the true self - remained elusive. I desperately wanted to rid myself of the useless negative "masks" that plagued my life and find my so-called true self. I kept on running into people who quoted the Temple of Apollo at Delphi - "Know Thyself." When I asked them what it meant they generally went into rambling gobbledeygook which lost me and I figured they didn't know either.

Gurdjieff kept on coming up too. "Remember Yourself." What did that mean? Someone said the Russian philosopher had developed powerful tools for tearing down something that he called the False Personality. I plunged enthusiastically into "The Fourth Way" and discovered that eliminating the False Personality is an essential task if one is to free the True Self from its prison of habits, associations, identifications, assumptions and limitations.

Gurdjieff makes it clear that things like anger and the many other aspects of the personality will not dissolve on their own. A new base, a new foundation, a new house must be rebuilt for a True Self that can live in total freedom.

One problem with the Gurdjieff and Ouspensky books: Written in the early part of the 20th century, the reading becomes laborious. Then I discovered that Vernon Howard, Jean Kline, and Eckhart Tolle had translated the ancient teachings of the Aryans, the Sufis and Gurdjieff.

Over the years I read and re-read the teachings, practiced what they taught, conducted workshops and classes, and eventually discovered the need for a simple, effective method for people to find their own way to freedom from the False Self. I cracked the Glass Darkly. This is that book. Enjoy!

Oh, an afterthought: Yes, the Hindu Yogi was right on. "You will go to the far side of the Americas – you will come back through the darkness into the light and you will know and understand the meaning of the One Self – that which is the true self within you."

Robert
Millens Bay, Cape Vincent, NY
September 2007

1

BREAKING FREE.
SEARCHING FOR THE TRUE SELF

"The spirit is the true self, not that physical figure which can be pointed out by your finger." — Cicero

Throughout the ages, the teachings of the ancients have echoed through the mystery schools of China, Tibet, India, the Middle East and Europe. The message? There is a release from suffering and desperation. There is a way out.

For many people life is like riding a helter-skelter roller coaster that never ends, never stands still. The ride becomes boring and relief is found in excessive drinking, eating, watching television, not because people want to, but because many don't know how to stop the roller coaster. They don't know how to get off.

An estimated one million people a day phone in sick, and some media surveys discovered that some 87 % of Americans dislike their jobs. Besides hating their jobs, and some even becoming workaholics, many people dwell on hopes that tomorrow is going to be brighter. Many dwell on winning a lottery.

The stress of the roller-coaster is undermining our social structure. In 2005, married couples became a minority of all American households for the first time,

Home life with a spouse is just as bad, which is why the US Census Bureau reported that in 2005 51 per cent of women said they were living without a spouse. The tired and worn scenario of married life is no longer appealing: a spouse mentions a loaded trigger word – bills, weight, tiredness, mother or work. That launches a rerun of an old, terribly worn argument. Afterwards you wonder "Why do we have to go through all this again and again?" No one seems to notice that the dialogue was exactly the same as yesterday, last week, last month, and before that.

Life on the roller coaster can destroy or cripple you physically and mentally. Roller coaster syndrome includes fatigue, indigestion, chest pain, shortness of breath, nervous tics or dizziness. Behavioral signs may include temper outbursts, restlessness, insomnia, difficulty relaxing, irritability, impatience, forgetfulness, difficulty concentrating, boredom and mood swings from euphoria to depression. And then there is insomnia.

The roller coaster rider can lie awake at night unable to sleep while a seemingly never ending stream of mind-chatter floods the mind. The doctor gives "something to help," but you wake up feeling numb with no enthusiasm for life. In desperation, you consider drinking more alcohol, finding a "friend" at the office, something, anything that will get you off your own pet roller coaster.

So you join the "Y" and learn Hatha Yoga. An acquaintance senses your desperation. "There is a solution," they tell you. "It's called enlightenment. Empowering your True Self. It's your way out."

"True Self?" you exclaim. "I am my true self. It's the hum-drum, tedious life that's killing me. I wake up anxious and tired. I look out the window and the damned world is still there – ugly, fearful and filled with stressed people."

"That's not your True Self – that's the Mechanical Self," says your acquaintance. "You've been trained to respond.

Over the next little while, your friend reveals how you can dissolve that Mechanical Self and bring out your True Self. In addition you will learn how to stop living in the past and live in the Here and Now. Also, you will learn to love yourself unconditionally.

You shrug. "Sounds like magic. I don't go to church but I like to think I am a spiritual person."

The acquaintance laughs. "Discovering and empowering your True Self is not religion. When you learn and practice these things, they will enhance your spirituality a thousand fold."

You race home and excitedly tell your spouse what you have learned.

"You're nuts! They used to burn people at the stake for less. Who did you meet? A witch?"

Hurt and puzzled because of people's reactions, but determined to discover more about what you have learned, you decide to press on. Quickly, you learn that your spouse's ego – the Mechanical Self – felt threatened. Which is why she responded the way she did. The roller coaster is starting to slow down. In a moment, it will stop.

To discover your own True Self you need two key elements: Desire and Passion. Desire is the intent, the journey or the way as the Taoists call it. Passion is the fire, the energy, the burning desire to succeed. This may seem strange in the journey ahead, because you will find yourself with the passion to do absolutely nothing. Many things in these teachings are complete reversals of what you have been trained to think.

STOP WHAT YOU ARE DOING

Take a slow deep breath, hold it for a moment, then as you breathe out say aloud the words: "Wide awake!" Now, read this section and then put the book down, you can come back to it shortly.

Right now, be aware of where you are. At home, in an office, a restaurant, sitting in a car. Be aware of where you are, and your place in that environment. Feel your body pressing on whatever you are resting on. Feel the clothes on your body. Be conscious of the shoes on your feet. Observe what your hands are doing. Notice your breathing. Listen to the sounds around you. Be aware.

While you were reading the book, you probably had no thought for yourself. You were reading but you had no conscious awareness of the fact you were reading. But now, you are suddenly aware of a different form of consciousness. You turned the searchlight of awareness upon yourself. This is called Self Remembering.

Now, go one step further. Observe yourself as you watch yourself. Observe any thoughts that pass through your head. Resist commenting, simply watch.

When you are in this state of awareness, you are free. If you didn't realize it, when you were being aware of where you are, what you were wearing, what you were feeling, you were totally in the present, in the Here and Now. For a few moments, you have been off the roller coaster.

Now, continue with the book so that you can learn how to get off the roller coaster and stay off forever.

LOOKING THROUGH A GLASS DARKLY

The idea that human beings are mechanically minded is far from new. The mechanical mind is not with young children, it develops as we start to grow. Paul of Tarsus noted this when he wrote: *"When I was a child, I spoke as a child, I understood as a child, I thought as a child: but when I became a man, I put away childish things. For now we see through a glass darkly."* (KGB 1 Corinthians 13)

A glass darkly! The prison. The containment area. The dungeon. Plato created his famous prisoners-in-the-cave allegory which was told by his student, Socrates.

A group of prisoners was kept chained in a dark cave. They huddled round a fire for warmth and security. Security? They were afraid. They feared the looming, eerie figures on the walls of the cave – dark, menacing figures, who always seemed to watch them.

One day, one of the prisoners broke free from his mental chains and bravely climbed the rocks where he made a startling discovery: the dark, menacing figures on the walls were nothing more than the prisoners' own shadows. Before he could announce this startling discovery, he spotted a shaft of light. He pushed upward and climbed through a hole. Suddenly, he was outside the cave and in open country. Here was sunlight! Meadows! Trees! Birds! Fresh air!

Overjoyed, he scrambled back into the cave and announced his discovery.

Screaming abuse, the prisoners showered him with stones. "Fraud! You're crazy! Full of lies!" they cried. "You're beset by the Devil!" Sadly, the man hastily retreated back to the outside world and his new freedom, leaving the people in the cave to believe in their illusions, their smug assumptions that what they saw in the shadows and believed was real.

Blaise Pascal wrote: "Human life is thus only an endless illusion. Men deceive and flatter each other. No one speaks of us in our presence as he does when we are gone. Society is based on mutual hypocrisy."

In this world of illusions people are frightened. They feel insecure. They feel frustrated by their inability to find happiness. They watch the "dark, menacing figures" on their own walls – loneliness, sickness, isolation, violence, and death – a montage of fears rebuilt and intensified daily as they watch their window on the world – television! They add another lock on their doors and secure the windows with bars – hardly thinking that in keeping the "dark, menacing figures" outside, they are building their own prison, their own cave.

In spite of all these illusions, there is a way out and it's been known and used for centuries. It's the greatest secret on Earth. It is beyond Paul's "glass darkly," far away from the Cave, and it is the last place most human beings think of looking. It's within. "Heaven is within you," said that great teacher Jesus. "Peace that passes all understandings," a note always attributed to the mystical Jesus, dates back many centuries.

THE MOVING FINGER WRITES

Many archeologists and some anthropologists probing the origin of cave paintings in prehistoric Europe are concluding that men and women, even though it was so long ago, sensed or realized that there was and is something else beyond their ordinary lives. Some people

13

call it mystical thinking, some call it cosmic thinking. Whatever it is, the consensus is a Higher Power, within and without.

The Aryans, the tribes that mysteriously emerged out of nowhere and settled in India some 10,000 years ago, knew all about mystical thinking. Some say they originated with the Lemurians, others claim they came from beyond the skies. One thing was clearly evident: They knew there was a marked difference between the two Selves that exist in human beings – the Negative Self and the True Self.

Over the centuries, perhaps through evolution, perhaps through neglect, the mystical teachings were largely forgotten. But somehow, a thread of this philosophy was kept, cherished and guarded in the mystery schools that survived in the desserts or the high mountains away from civilization.

One group of Aryan mystics moved to Persia, now Iran, and they became known as the Sufis – the wool gatherers. They found the protective umbrella of Islam where their mystical philosophies were developed and perfected.

The essence of these great and unique mystical teachings is that the Negative Self, the False Self, the mechanical Ego can be systematically eliminated, and the True Self, the Higher Self can be brought into the fore. Paul's "glass darkly" can be cleaned and removed. The prison bars and the illusions disappear and in their place the flower of the True Self blooms.

Over the centuries Sufi philosophers and writers helped to further the True Self thinking. In The Rubaiyat of Omar Khayyam (1859) we read: *The Moving Finger writes; and, having writ, Moves on; nor all thy Piety nor Wit shall lure it back to cancel half a Line, Nor all thy Tears wash out a Word of it.*

Many people have discussed the meaning. A favorite of the mechanical minds is: Whatever you do in your life is your responsibility and cannot be changed. Actually there is. What can be changed is the way you see it. The mystical power of understanding, as we shall see.

This is one of the great truths: *"Nothing is what it seems because you have the power to change the way you see it."*

As descendants of the Aryans migrated west into the Middle East, north Africa and Europe, the seeds of mystical thinking flourished among secret schools and sects. The message was simple. There is a new life, men and women can embrace a new way of living not only for this life, but in the Hereafter. Various leaders taught the principles of mystical thinking, and many risked their lives, and indeed lost their lives for teaching True Self philosophy.

Lao-Tse the founder of Taoism, a student of Confucius, never had books and always taught from his mind. He promoted Here-and-Now intuitive action.

Buddha observed the stress and sufferings in humanity and taught the basic elements of discovering the True Self.

Immanuel Kant credited Scottish philosopher David Hume with awakening him from "dogmatic slumber" and later wrote a treatise on Enlightenment in which he blamed the church for "people's inability to think for themselves." Kant also bravely accused the church of laying aside the teachings of Jesus in favor of implementing church ritual. It brought down the wrath of the King of Prussia.

When Dutch philosopher, Benedict Spinoza taught higher learning, authorities attempted to bribe him to cease his teachings. When he refused, he was excommunicated and an attempt made to kill him.

In his writings, which were suppressed for many years, Jacob Boehme said *"Whosoever is desirous to attain to Divine Vision in himself, and to speak with God in Christ, let him follow this Course, and he shall attain it."*

Boehme also triggered explosive controversy when he said that Heaven and Hell exist only within a person, a key teaching of mysticism. Boehme crossed into Spirit in 1642. Three and a half centuries later – September 1999 – the New York Times carried a Vatican story confirming that Hell was not a place, but a personal "state of being." It gives new meaning to the old adage: *"Know the truth, and the truth shall set you free."* Sometimes the truth, revealed at the wrong moment will get you killed.

REWARDS VERSUS DANGERS

The path to Mysticism, the journey to empowering the True Self is not an easy one, but as many pilgrims, many explorers have discovered, the rewards infinitely outweigh the dangers from non-believers.

The journey to the True Self involves self change. It involves exploration, understanding and awareness. It is an acquisition of knowledge, but more than acquisition, it involves the understanding of Self. It is working with Self-insight without the contamination of judging. We live in a world that bathes in the mire of judging. Resist it. This is critically important. Never judge anything you do in spiritual exploration – work to understand what you are doing.

If you read the "New Age" magazines you will realize that many, many people are in search of spirituality, their higher selves. George Barna of Barna Research in California which specializes in trends of the mainline churches, said in 2006 that people are leaving the churches in search of God. People are coming to understand the irony that there is little or no spirituality in the mainline churches.

Thus many people are attending workshops, seminars, development circles, classes in search of enlightenment, their higher selves, seeking that mystical connection with God, the Creator, the Source of their Being.

Paul Solomon the spiritual teacher from Virginia Beach once declared that you can tell a person who has had a mystical experience with God – a higher power – because that person has changed. The mystics declare that once you have found your True Self, the old you disappears. It fades into oblivion.

THE HUMAN MINDS

Thaddeus Golas in his small but magnificent work, "The Lazy Man's Guide to Enlightenment" wrote: *"Whatever you are doing, love yourself for doing it."* In doing workshops we often echo these words by saying: *Whatever you do in your life, love yourself for doing it and you will always do the right thing.*

You may protest and exclaim: "But that is impossible!" Examine your response and you will find all your excuses hail from the old mechanical, conditioned self. So it's time to understand why we do things and how the duality of Self comes into being.

You have a Conscious Mind and a Sub-conscious mind. The Conscious Mind comes into existence when you wake up in the morning, and it disappears when you go to sleep at night. The Conscious Mind is critically important in your life: It guides you through the day, makes judgments, analyzes events and makes key decisions. It's much like the captain of a ship. The captain makes executive decisions -- speed, course, destination and takes other key initiatives. The real work on board takes place below deck. In the human body, below deck is the realm of the Sub-conscious Mind.

The Sub-conscious looks after your breathing, your heart, your digestive system, your immune system and more. The Sub-conscious Mind is the general manager of your body. It constantly communicates with every cell in your body and processes 100,000 bits of information every second of every day. It never sleeps. It monitors your environment even when you think you are totally asleep. This is a great reason why you should never go to sleep on the couch with your television blazing away. The Sub-conscious listens to all those commercials, and you sleep on, completely unaware of what is being recorded in your memory banks. Even when you wake up you have no idea why you have a distinct desire for a burger or a pizza. You have been programmed.

The Sub-conscious has been compared to a biological computer. It is stunningly powerful with tremendous capabilities, and most people fail to use more than just a slim margin of its capabilities.

The Sub-conscious Mind records everything we do. It remembers everything. The more emotional energy involved with an incident, the greater impression is made on the Sub-Conscious. This biological computer remembers when you first met that special person in your life, the day you graduated school, the day you first went to school. It remembers the day you first walked and who was around to witness the event. It also remembers how your mother felt the day you were born.

Impossible? Daniel Levitin in "This Is Your Brain On Music" relates an interesting phenomenon. Scientific experiments have shown that if you repeatedly play a particular piece of music close to a mother's womb, and then never play the music again until the baby is one year old, then play a selection of music including the piece played before birth, the infant will be drawn to the music of the womb. It does not matter whether the music is classical or popular. Such experiments clearly demonstrate that the Sub-conscious Mind is already recording memories before the birth of a child. The Sub-conscious Mind is a powerhouse of memories.

REFRAMING AN ANCIENT MEMORY

Mary, an enthusiastic 60-year-old joined one of my spiritual development classes in British Columbia. As we sat in meditation, it became obvious she had a problem – a distracting hiccup about every thirty seconds. Later, I asked her about it. "I've had it for years. My mother told me the doctor said it started when I suffered an illness when I was four years old," she said. "I hope it doesn't bother anyone in the class."

Mary had suffered with this afflicton for 56 years—at least, that's what she believed from what the doctor told her. She came for hypnotherapy and we regressed her Sub-conscious Mind. We went back to the four years – yes, the hiccup was there. Then we found out it did not start at four: It began much earlier. We asked the Sub-conscious to take us back to the originating memory, the root cause.

Suddenly, Mary was conscious of the day she was born. Her voice thinned. She was struggling for air. I detached her from the memory so she could witness it in emotionless black and white without suffering the rigors of suffocation. Mary talked of several dedicated doctors working to restore her breathing and finally recalled being in a circular tube.

Later, as her mother had crossed into Spirit, she checked with an older brother. "Yes, I recall there was trouble when you were born. You lived in an oxygen tent for several days before you were allowed to come home. They said you were born with the umbilical chord round your neck."

In hypnosis, we took Mary back to her birth, reframed the full memory by erasing the original, and replacing it with a normal birth delivery with the umbilical chord in its correct place. When Mary came out of hypnosis, the hiccup with which she had suffered for 60 years was gone. In hypnosis this technique is called reframing.

CREATING THE CONDITIONED MIND

The Sub-conscious Mind records everything you see, everything you touch, taste, hear and feel in your mind and body. It continually monitors your personal world, and never misses an action or the emotions connected with that action, in fact the higher the degree of emotion, the more intense is the recording. I have had clients who complained: "I have a terrible memory." So I explained: "You have an excellent memory. Your problem is accessing it. There's no such thing as a bad memory."

Have you ever wondered why you are the way you are? The way you react when someone says something or when something goes wrong? You know you are angry or jealous or fearful and when you stop to consider yourself, you wonder where these embarrassing actions originate. Truth is, you learned these responses from someone or something in your past. The source could have been rooted with your parents, guardians, brothers, sisters, relatives, teachers, acquaintances at school, friends, lovers or someone you met on some avenue of life. They have all contributed in some measure to the way your Sub-conscious Mind views or reacts to your world.

Today, right now, you have a Subconscious Mind that is the sum total of all that you have ever done in your life. It's called the Conditioned Mind or the Mechanical Mind. In essence it is an

19

acquired mass of opinions, beliefs, contradictions and mechanical reactions that include habits, sensitivities, and yes, allergies. Your Sub-conscious Mind responds to everything, on cue. It's like a robot and is totally mechanical.

Exercise: The Lemon

Take a few moments from reading and do the following exercise. Do it slowly. Gently close your eyes and imagine you have a big, fat, yellow, juicy lemon on a board in front of you. You have a sharp knife. Cut through the lemon, and watch as the juice squirts out of that big, fat, juicy lemon. Then, take one of the halves and cut it into quarters. Watch again as the juice dribbles out. Now, lift one of those quarters to you mouth and sink your teeth into it. Pause a few moments, then open your eyes.

You probably puckered up or at least felt more saliva in your mouth. But there wasn't a lemon there at all, was there? You imagined it. Now here's a fascinating point. With all its incredible latent powers, the Sub-conscious Mind does not know the difference between reality and something imagined. As Sigmund Freud once suggested, if it comes to a battle between reality and the imagination, the imagination will always win.

It's important to understand that the imagination can only work on something or things that are already known: memories collected and preserved by the Sub-conscious.

On what is all imagination based? It is based on something known, that is, a memory or memories of something experienced outside of one's self. Imagination is always based on memories and thoughts are based on those memories. If you are asked to imagine a lemon, the resulting thoughts are based on your experiences of the fruit. If you were asked to imagine God, your visualized projection would be based on various memories picked up in your life. Imagination and the subconscious mind are therefore robotic, in other words – the Mechanical Mind, the Conditioned Mind.

One interesting fact that many people fail to acknowledge is that the subconscious mind with all its powers, does not know the difference between right and wrong. Think about this.

If the subconscious mind had the capability of right and wrong recognition, it would not let people smoke cigarettes, become obese or take dangerous drugs. This is in spite of the fact that the subconscious mind contains programming designed to ensure its survival.

MEMORIES FUEL THE FALSE SELF

The False Self, the Mechanical Mind, the Human Ego is based on functional memory. Each of its faces – anger, jealousy, bitterness, revenge and the rest – are based on memory and designed as a concept, a program, a tool. Some faces of the False Self are powerful, others are less powerful. The Ego has a heirarchy, just like a government or church organization. There are top dogs, support dogs, aides that serve the support dogs, and then lots of less powerful dogs.

The False Self is almost totally predictable. It has conceptual programming which in the Mechanical Mind becomes a dominant habit, and a blind or unconscious laziness easily sets it. Creativity, learning, exploring new thoughts, new philosophies, the desire to adventure and discover are put on a person's back burner. There is comfort and security in the rut of the Mechanical Mind and the Ego stays king, president, dictator, pope, archbishop or top dog.

This will explain why many people, particularly men, are totally controlled by a top dog ego and stay entrenched while the whole world evolves. People lose childhood sensitivities about the age of eight and the Ego develops and comes to the fore. Organs atrophy, and intuitive abilities and creative instincts fail. Women are more inclined to see through the illusions of Ego and develop their own spirituality. The more a woman aligns with a man's world, the more subject she is to adopt a male Mechanical Mind.

Paul's Glass Darkly is much in evidence.

IMAGINING THE TRUE SELF

At this point, you may be attempting to imagine or wonder what your Higher Self, your True Self is like. Resist the attempt.

While the Sub-conscious is very useful for doing every-day things in an every-day environment, such as toiletry and domestic chores, routine work, shopping, writing reports, driving a car, and interacting with others—most of which are actions done without our being aware of what we are doing. We know what we are doing, but we are not aware.

But imagining your True Self? This may come as a surprise but the Conditioned Mind, the Mechanical Mind cannot penetrate the Spiritual World. Depending upon its conditioning and conceptual programming, memories and old learning may be limiting, forming a wall that blocks. The Mechanical Mind may hold various views, sometimes negative on such areas as consciousness, awareness, esoteric thinking, and it may well have heard about the True Self in conversation, on televison or on the internet. But to imagine what it might be like in truth?

As we tread the mystic path, a key lesson here is: Never make imaginative assumptions as to the nature of your Higher Self, your True Self. Allow it to surprise you.

The Conditioned Mind is the keeper of your beliefs, and believe it or not, you are limited by your own beliefs. Can you imagine yourself driving through countryside you have never seen before, and saying to yourself: "I know I'm not going to like what I see in the next valley," or "This journey is going to be boring." Such assumptions and judgments spring from the old Conditioned Mind. Many people in search of the True Self, the Higher Self, assume they know what the True Self is like. Resist judging and allow it to surprise you. The old adage "Expect the unexpected" is never more meaningful than when one is exploring the Higher Self.

Exercise: Stop Judging For A While

Decide not to judge, cast an opinion, criticize anyone, including yourself for one hour. Then observe how you feel. You may be pleasantly surprised.

Part One: For a start, when you have a quiet moment to yourself, stand or sit in front of a mirror and observe yourself without judgment, comment or criticism. Simply observe how you are both inside and out. Observe your eyes, your hair, skin, facial formation, the way your shoulders sit. Observe your body as it breathes in and out. Observe your inner feelings. If you realize any stressful areas, observe them – and do it without judgment, criticism, comment. Simply observe. If any unusual emotions are stirred, observe them too. Observe everything.

Part Two: Call someone on the telephone, someone you may not necessarily see eye to eye with. Conduct a conversation and be aware of what you are saying. Be an observer, a watcher of your own actions, feelings and voice. Observe any natural inclination to judge or be critical.

When you have finished both of these parts, sit down and observe how you feel in body and mind. You may be pleasantly surprised at how you handled the False Self. Impartial observation is a key strategy in defeating the False Self.

THE TWO SELVES WITHIN

Work to understand this basic principle and see if this applies to you.

A person lives with two selves: Self #1 which is the False Self, and Self #2 which is the True Self. Grasping this basic fact is sometimes difficult, but perseverance will bring its rewards.

Self #1 is the False Self, the Persona the face mask that consists of everything negative within a person. It produces Mechanical Thinking often negative in nature. These negativities manifest with different intensities or faces in each person. Do you recognize any of these within you? There can be hundreds, perhaps thousands in one person.

They include: *envy, helplessness, posturing, jealousy, anger, arrogance, deceit, discontent, despair, deviousness, anguish, lying, worry, fear, panic, criticism, bitterness, revenge, tension, boredom, resistance, foolishness, confusion, flattery, conceit, insecurity, ignorance, possession, obsession, boastfulness, self-condemnation, terror and hatred.*

The first step to taking the path to the True Self is by recognizing the faces of the False Self. Mull over these words and you may quickly realize these conditions, these faces do not contribute to your well being in any way. In fact they detract from your well being, sometimes with devastating impact. Consider the ramifications jealousy and anger have had on the world. Whole nations have gone to war on these two faces alone.

Religions refer to the False Self as the Devil within us, and psychologists describe it as the Ego-Self that clings to and lives in an illusion. Whatever you want to call it, Self #1 is the cause of all negative pressures within us, and when out of control, explodes causing a multitude of problems in our world.

A person dominated by Self #1 does not live or enjoy life. He or she is hounded by the many faces of the Ego-Self such as bitterness, revenge, jealousy, and possession. They are given to frequent and automatic angers and terrified by an imagination fueled by negative fears.

The worst part is the dominated person frequently identifies with these negative faces because he or she incorrectly assumes they are Self #1. "That's the way I am. I can't change," is the lame excuse. The big mistake so many people make however, including government, the judiciary, many mental health practitioners and therapists, is believing Self #1 can be changed or reformed by mechanical or conditioned thinking.

Many anger management sessions work to suppress the symptoms of the False Self, but sooner or later, often sooner, the symptoms – the faces of the False Self return with a vengeance. It is totally useless to try and suppress the negative ego. Self #1 will defend itself and make an array of impressive promises it cannot keep. It is like asking the habitually fast driver who keeps breaking the speed limit to police himself.

THE BARRIER TO HAPPINESS

Self #1 is your barrier to happiness. All happiness created by Self #1 is temporary and unsatisfying. You go to a party and meet a wonderful human being – "My soul mate" you think happily. You are on cloud nine. Life is suddenly great. You exude happiness. The sensation is warm and wonderful. You hastily imagine your life with this new soul mate. You run imaginative and exotic mental-movies that thrill your entire mind and body. The end of the party comes. Suddenly you spot your soul mate disappearing with another. Aghast! Your vision crashes. You feel totally helpless. Angry and hurt, you stagger away, completely deflated. You lose yourself in alcohol and wake up next day with the world's worst hangover. You wonder how you could have been so stupid. "When is this roller coaster going to stop," you might mutter.

Self #1 is not only a barrier to true, lasting happiness, it can also undermine your health, your career, your relationships, your family life and many other aspects. The person – man or woman – dominated by Self #1 does not live their lives, they are driven and pushed. They are helpless victims riding the eternal roller coaster.

The more power that society gives a person dominated by Self #1, the more destructive he or she can be. Witness the rampant abuse of children by the clergy, wars around the world, rebellions, and murder and assassinations. Politicians and people in show business frequently find it difficult to control the energy manifested by the negative ego.

Remember: Self #1 is the product of the Conditioned Mind, the Mechanical Mind and it only exists as an illusion. It is not the true you.

English artist and mystic William Blake wrote: *"If the doors of perception were cleansed everything would appear to man as it is, infinite. For man has closed himself up, till he sees all things thru' chinks of his cavern."*

How does the Self # 1 – the False Self – come to exist? Zen philosopher Alan Watts wrote: *"Other people teach us who we are. Their attitudes to us are the mirror in which we learn to see ourselves, but the mirror is distorted."*

MAN OF A THOUSAND FACES

Back In the era of silent movies there was a great actor named Lon Chaney. People called him "The Man of a Thousand Faces", due to his uncanny ability to transform himself into many types of characters through makeup and pantomime. Ironically he went through agony to play many of the roles.

The idea that a person could have a thousand faces might sound far fetched, but some mystics and philosophers believe the average man and woman has numbers of False Self faces far in excess of one thousand.

Everything centers on that one critically important one-letter word "I". The mechanical man or woman does not and cannot have a permanent I. His or her I changes as quickly as their thoughts, feelings and moods. The Mechanical man or woman makes the mistake of considering themselves always the one and the same person, little realizing that in reality they are rapidly moving from I to I, face to face with the passing of each moment.

Gurdjieff said: "Man has no permanent and unchangeable I." As a person moves through every thought, mood, desire, sensation, the "I" is expressed, and the person makes the profound mistake of believing that he or she is always the same person. This explains that age-old problem of why people make decisions on future plans and frequently fail to carry them out.

"The whole never expresses itself, for the simple reason that it exists, as such, only physically as a thing, and in the abstract as a concept," he said. "Man has no individual I. But there are, instead, hundreds and thousands of separate small I's, very often entirely unknown to one another."

It's like an actor who frequently changes masks on a stage to play different characters. These faces, these I's never come into contact with one another because each one comes and dominates our figure, and then is completely replaced by another face, another I. Not only do they not come into contact with one another, they can be quite hostile to each other, maintaining an aloof exclusiveness and incompatibility. Each minute of waking consciousness the man and woman are saying or thinking "I", and each time the "I" is different. Some "I"s are stronger than others, based upon the accumulated knowledge and belief systems of the speaker. Strong "I"s in a person's personality are created by such environments as education, employment, religion, social contacts, relationships, being online, and watching television.

RECOGNIZE THE "I" IN THINGS WE DO

If you think about it, we use the "I" in most of the things we do, say and feel. And the interesting point is we use the "I"s without being conscious of the fact. There are many faces. The problem is we only know ourselves in relation to something. I am late for work. I feel stressed. I enjoy reading a book. I hate cereal. The "I" is always used in relationship to something.

Even the hackneyed phrase "I am" has no meaning on its own. Various organizations have built services based on the supposedly mystical values of "I Am," principally because when Moses (Exodus 3/14) asks God for his name, the response was "I AM THAT I AM." Hence millions of people dwell on the first two and the last two words. In fact, the key word is in the middle – "THAT." How?

If we turn to the Hindu philosophies we discover that the ancient Sages defined the Ultimate Reality by the Sanskrit word "TAT," from which the English word "THAT" is derived. TAT and its English equivalent are still used to designate, but not to describe, the Hindu idea of the Ultimate Reality behind the Phenomenal Universe. Thus is the myth of "I am."

The many faces of the Ego expressed by the "I" have no foundation and no constancy. The faces are all based on memories contained within the Sub-Conscious Mind, and there is no single face, no single individual in charge. The faces are all based on memories we have acquired in our lives. If you quietly observe yourself while engaged in a heated argument, you will probably hear your parents or grandparents speaking through you.

The ancient Eastern teachings compare a man or a woman to a house in which there are multitudes of servants but no master in the shape of a butler or even a chief executive officer. The servants have no knowledge of their duties, in fact not one of the staff has any idea of what they should be doing for the good of the house. Everyone wants to be in charge and it is this kind of chaos that threatens the very safety of the house.

One day, one servant who has received executive training, manages to take over and organizes some of the more sensible servants into a task force which brings order to the other levels of servants. The executive servant maintains control until the arrival of the owner of the house.

Whatever you want to call it, Self #1, the ego, the so-called "I" is the cause of all negative pressures within us, and when out of control, explodes causing a multitude of problems in our life and in the world.

And when you think about it all, you recognize that the "I" is totally meaningless, in fact it is a dangerous illusion.

THE DANGERS OF IDENTIFYING WITH THOUGHTS

The False Self is a master of manipulation. It creates an aura of reality around your thoughts. You may feel they are essential, imperative, totally necessary, and that your life would be lost without them.

Compulsive thinking, obsessive thinking, particularly when you wish to be somewhere else, can be stressful, debilitating and trigger chronic conditions in the body. Yet, so many people say they would feel guilty if they did not follow the rituals, the dogmas that Mechanical Society has taught them.

The interesting thing is that when you offer to show people how to escape interminable mind-chatter, compulsive thinking, they frequently think, sometimes openly, that the solution is fraudulent, that they will lose their sanity and security. Unknowingly, this is the voice of the False Self attempting to protect its domain – a domain that doesn't exist. It is a total illusion.

For many, compulsive thinking, obsessive thinking is their security. They are back in the cave. Back on the roller-coaster.

Sooner or later, these false illusions will crumble with the manifestation of the True Self. Illusions have no place in the realm of the True Self, the Higher Self.

THE MYSTICAL TRUE SELF

Self #2 – the True Self is also known as the Inner Self, the Higher Self or the Superconsciousness. It is the spirit force, the higher intelligence within us that works and operates without any conscious effort. It is the silent operator. It is within us always. It is the life force, the power that operates the central nervous system, the brain and other parts of the body and, for the most part, we rarely think about it. It is only when there is a malfunction – a deficiency or absence of positive energy – and negativity sets in that we experience the message in the form of pain or disabilities.

It is also the love force that is reflected in every cell in our bodies. This is the one most important reason that we should love ourselves unconditionally as we will explain in the third section of this book.

The True Self has all the qualities we admire in lovable people. These qualities include unconditional love, compassion, truth, happiness, strength and dedication. The True Self is the very essence of your Spirit – the essential you. It is entirely free of all negative emotions such as panic and despair.

The True Self has tremendous capacity for seeing everything clearly. There is no "glass darkly" in the realm of the True Self. Everything is crystal clear. You were born the True Self. It is never lost, never suffers from materialism but for many people, it is dominated and over-shadowed by the False Self, the Mechanical Mind. It is hidden behind Paul's glass darkly.

KILLING THE EGO, THE FALSE SELF

Some readers may be pleased to know that the False Self, the Negative Ego expires with the death of a person. It's one of the difficult phenomena to understand in spirit communications. I have worked as an intuitive and a medium with the ability to converse with spirits – loved ones who have crossed over – for almost 30 years.

It never ceases to amaze both mediums and the people for whom they are reading, how the personality of spirits can change once they have made their transition into the Spirit World.

"That can't be my Dad," says a young woman. "My father was always angry, unhappy and totally inconsiderate, and now you're trying to tell me he's lost all those nasty habits."

A male energy comes through and tells his widow: "I want you to know I love you." The widow shakes her head vigorously. "We were married for 51 years and not once did Henry tell me he loved me. Why is he doing this now?"

As you may well imagine, it is a very difficult development for a person who has lived in a False Self environment to understand. The simple fact is that when people make their transition into the Spirit World they lose much of the negative ego. As entities with pure consciousness, they are suddenly in a position to see their negative ego-selves stripped away. They realize how unproductive their negative egos were in their lives. They review their life on Earth clearly and they recognize their True Selves. No one judges you in the Spirit World or Heaven, you simply see the light of truth. It is the Light of Realization.

This is not something new. Some 2,300 years ago Plato wrote in his prison play—Phaedo: *"And then the foolishness of the body will be cleared away and we shall be pure and hold converse with other pure souls, and know of ourselves the clear light everywhere; and this is surely the light of truth."*

If this happens — and we must assume it does — why cannot people have the ability to strip their bodies and minds of the ego-self while they are here on Earth? Why can't people release themselves and see the light of truth ahead of time? Why cannot people enjoy their lives before they make their transition into the next life? Well the good news is — you can and this book will start you on the path.

The Upanishads, the sacred literature of India describe the True Self this way: "The Self knows all, is not born, does not die, is not the effect of any cause; is eternal, self-existent, imperishable..."

In western society, the True Self is part of the Heaven within. It knows itself. It has no illusions. It is difficult to describe in words because it is beyond the realm of comparison.

Consider this. How do you convey the fire and passion of a symphony to someone who cannot hear? How do you explain the beauty of a gorgeous sunset to a person who cannot see? The True Self is an experience, an elevated vibration. Once you are on that vibration, the dominating False Self is gone and you are free.

THE TRUE SELF: AN INEFFABLE EXPERIENCE

It is on this level, this vibration that you can easily communicate meaningfully with God, the Creator, saints, guardian angels, spirit guides and loved ones in spirit. There is no shame, no feeling of guilt, no memory of "sin," you simply communicate and share the mystical experience. Many mystics refer to knowing and being the True Self as an ineffable experience.

A young psychology student asked me in a workshop: "What's wrong with stress and anger management? All the negatives in a human can be controlled and even suppressed."

Management techniques are nothing but temporary blocks sustained by will power, I told her. When attention moves elsewhere, the techniques and will fail. The ego - the False Self - comprises a vast collection of memories and each memory has a character, a face, a personality, and with that come set thoughts, set actions which you project mechanically. This is why a person who is defending a negative face will repeat the same words with very little variation. Sayings are habitual, and it is habit that makes them appear permanent. A person who is dominated by Self #1, the False Self really believes they cannot change. Their ego-centered mind fears change, and in this way condemns the person to a life in the cave, or looking through the glass darkly.

There is a key to breaking free.

THE SECRET FOR SHEDDING THE FALSE SELF

It is well to remember, Self #1, which is the False Self, is non-existent, but by believing in it, we act as if it were real. In truth, there is only one self - Self # 2, the True Self.

As we explained earlier, Self #1 cannot be changed, suppressed or reformed. It cannot be "managed" or "converted" as some mainstream mental health practitioners claim, but it can be dissolved, and this is done by shining the Light of Awareness on its face.

Negatives always avoid the light. They feel drawn to working in the dark. Darkness is their strength, their security. Evil lurks in darkness. Movies depicting crime and gangsters are usually shrouded in darkness. Believe it or not, the False Self detests the light of awareness.

The challenge at this point is to shine the light of awareness on the many faces of the False Self, and free ourselves from the power of the old ways. This is done by dissolving the false, imaginery self and becoming attuned to the True Self.

How do we dissolve the negative faces of Self #1? It's a very effective, age-old technique called Impartial Self Observation.

This is another name for Awareness. Like the investigative light of journalists shining the light on criminals, the Light of Awareness is the mortal enemy of Self #1, the Ego-Self. The False Self cannot tolerate it and without any conscious direction or urging, the many faces of the Ego-Self start to dissolve. They start to diminish, and eventually they have no power at all.

Remember this truth: The False Self cannot be controlled or suppressed, but by shining the Light of Awareness, the faces will start to dissolve.

What are the faces? We mentioned some earlier, but they are worth repeating: They include:

Envy, helplessness, posturing, jealousy, anger, arrogance, deceit, discontent, despair, deviousness, anguish, lying, guilt, worry, fear, panic, criticism, bitterness, revenge, tension, boredom, resistance, foolishness, confusion, flattery, conceit, insecurity, ignorance, possession, obsession, boastfulness, self-condemnation, terror and hatred.

There are many more. Are you aware of any?

The interesting thing is that not one of these faces does a person any good, in fact most will cause either mental or physical harm, or both. The good news is that every one can be dissolved and removed from your life.

THE POWER OF IMPARTIAL SELF OBSERVATION

Dissolution does not happen en masse, it can happen one face at a time, or by simply dissolving one major face of the False Self, a whole stack of other faces may dissolve. It is much like a line of dominoes falling into one another. The dissolution of one major face may dissolve several others as it loses energy and fades away.

Impartial Self Observation or Selective Awareness comes about through a practice that has been known down the ages. It is a secret that should have been shared with millions of people many centuries ago. The practice of living with the True Self without the False Self could have averted many wars, many deaths, and much unhappiness in the world.

P.D. Ouspensky, student of and writer for the great philosopher, George Gurdjieff, wrote:

Self-observation brings man to the realization of the necessity for self-change. And in observing himself a man notices that self-observation itself brings about certain changes in his inner processes. He begins to understand that self-observation is an instrument of self-change, a means of awakening. By observing himself he throws, as it were, a ray of light onto his inner processes which have hitherto worked in complete darkness. And under the influence of this light the processes themselves begin to change.

Impartial Self Observation is the entrance, the pathway, the Gateway to a new sense of Self, the True Self.

When you use Impartial Self Observation to view the actions of Self #1, the False Self, without comment or criticism, you view the behavior in its true colors. You see and understand that the negative behavior, the negative face of Self #1 exists as an illusion. The True Self is above all this negativity.

J. Krishnamurti, the great Indian Spiritual philosopher explained Awareness this way:

"Awareness is observation without condemnation. Awareness brings understanding, because there is no condemnation or identification but silent observation. If I want to understand something, I must observe, I must not criticize, I must not condemn, I must not pursue it as pleasure or avoid it as non-pleasure. There must be silent observation of a fact."

Let us clarify this a step further.

When a person gets angry they normally react in the only way they know how–the way of the Conditioned or Mechanical Mind. Asked about it they may become indignant, flustered and declare: "I'm not angry," or "I deserve to be angry," or "He made me angry." The person demonstrating anger will perpetuate the anger and attempt to justify it, by bringing in the face of justification which only makes matters worse. He or she may claim they have a right to be angry. They cannot understand that anger is a self-punishing feature of Self #1, the False Self.

Anger is a learned or acquired behavior. In running the anger course, other faces of the negative Ego-Self will likely come up such as guilt, embarrassment, denial and exhaustion. Had the person applied the awareness technique during the burst of anger, it would have taken a a completely different course. Be aware and observe everything without judgment, comment, opinion etc.

Think about this point. All the negative faces of Self #1, the False Self, are caused by wrong viewpoints: anger, bitterness, resentment, jealousy, hatred, etc., and they do nothing for us. To let them run our lives is about as sensible as shooting ourselves in the feet.

Study all the faces of the Self #1 through Impartial Self Observation and they will start to dissolve–and you will be free.

WHY IS IT CALLED IMPARTIAL?

Impartiality is critical to the success of the process of discovering the power of the True Self. Recall the exercise earlier about viewing yourself through a mirror? You did it without judgment so it is vitally important to remember that Self Observation should always be conducted without comment, criticism, judgment, and an expression of opinion or feelings.

Otherwise it will be the old Self #1 intruding, and your outlook will be biased and ineffective. It would be like a shoplifter working for Security in the store that he or she is robbing.

Exercise: Observation Technique # 1

First of all, find a comfortable seat in a quiet place where you will not be disturbed. The practice of self-observation should be started in a small way so that you can understand and get the process working properly. Now, relax by focusing upon your breathing. Do not try to change anything, simply be conscious of your body breathing in and breathing out. Then perform the following.

1) *Be conscious of your head and in particular your mind. Imagine your consciousness is <u>a video camera </u>and it has the ability to watch you from outside your body. Imagine it is positioned about two feet above your head and about four feet in front of you, perhaps slightly to the right or left. It has you perfectly in focus. Work to achieve the positioning of the video camera.*

2) *Now, imagine seeing yourself from the camera's viewpoint. Remember, view yourself without criticism, opinion or comment. Be totally impartial. What do you see? Your body? How does it appear? Note the posture of your body. How does your body feel? Is there tension anywhere. Make a mental note, but make no comment. Have the camera take a look at your face, chest, legs and feet.*

3) *Do this for several minutes. Impartially observe yourself in everything you are doing. Then take a deep breath and terminate the exercise.*

4) *Afterwards, make a note of any reactions your body made while you were watching it. Did you feel any inclination to manifest a change. You may be surprised.*

5) *Perform this exercise several times until you are completely comfortable with the exercise. After sitting down for the first time, afterwards you can do it while performing simple tasks such as cleaning your teeth, making breakfast, walking along a street, or being at work. Initially, it should be done when you are in a fairly quiet sense of mind.*

CAUTION: Self #1 — the False Self — may interfere with some critical comment. If it does, observe impartially any thoughts, feelings, suggestions that pop up without comment and resume the exercise. You should know that the False Self will not be defeated easily.

Exercise: Observation Technique # 2

When you are confident with Observation Technique # 1, continue with this observation technique, preferably when you are alone doing some simple domestic chores, perhaps cleaning your teeth, having a shower, making the bed, dressing, eating a meal, or performing a quiet task around the home. Simply learn to watch yourself.

Check on how you feel, how your body is moving, how you are breathing, how your face feels, how you feel emotionally inside. Normally at this stage, the False Self will be quiet. It may prompt you with: "You know, all this is silly," or "This sort of stuff never works." Observe everything. Your thoughts, your movements, everything. And observe without comment, criticism or judgment. Observe what you learn or understand.

Practice this until you feel comfortable with it. Practice will bring about confidence in the techniques of impartial observation. When you feel you are becoming adept, quietly move onto the next exercise.

Exercise: Observation Technique # 3

One day you will find yourself in an unpleasant situation, generated either by yourself or involving someone else. Let us assume the other person is doing or saying something that causes you to react negatively. You have heard the dialogue before, but this time you will hear it differently.

Enter the Impartial Self-Observation mode and either using your imaginary video camera watch or your own mental ability watch everything you do at the physical and mental levels. Do not watch the other person or people. Observe yourself in everything that happens.

How do you feel? How are you reacting? What are your emotions? Is your stress level changing? What muscles are tightening in your body? Work to observe all these occurrences without comment, criticism or opinion.

When the situation has passed, observe to see if there are any changes. After doing this several times, notice how your attitudes and approaches to problems are changing. Always without comment, judgment, opinion, criticism.

OBSERVE WITHOUT JUDGING

As these techniques are practiced and become part of your daily routine, you may be disturbed by what you see or feel. Observe the changes or disturbances impartially. You may well find you are not the person you thought you were. Never judge yourself–simply observe these changes. You will notice negatives that you were sure did not exist in your makeup. If you feel alarmed, recognize the alarm as another face of the Ego-Self. It is nothing more than an old mechanical response.

When you see or feel changes happening to the False Self, you may be inclined to celebrate, throw a party, sing in exultation. Resist. Bring on the imaginary video camera: Observe these desires to celebrate and learn from them.

As you progress in Impartial Self Observation you will find yourself becoming more relaxed with more energy, you will become more focused, more confident, more creative and generally healthier than before. You may or may not be aware at this stage that you are working through your True Self.

Once you are comfortable with the video camera technique of self-observation, simply switch over to mentally watching yourself.

WHATEVER HAPPENS OBSERVE IT

We live in an opinionated world. Society has become so indoctrinated with opinions that not to have an opinion on something, particularly politics and government, is close to treason. So many people want to know what other people are thinking. It's not because other people really want to know how you feel, it's because most people are afraid of missing or losing something. They also take great comfort in knowing that you are on their side. It's a group security issue.

This is typical of the Mechanical Mind. It detests making decisions. It hates to be alone. It finds comfort in numbers. This explains why so many people in your life want to know how you feel about things. Their False Selves need the security of knowing they are not alone.

The False Self detests change. It nestles in the collection of countless memories it has acquired over the years. It projects its future based on existing memories. This is why when someone introduces an idea, a concept that is outside its parameters, the False Self will automatically show signs of resistance.

On the other hand, the True Self, even when apparently alone, provides strength at all times. It observes the strange neuroses of humanity and knows that one day everyone will dissolve that "glass darkly" – that False Self, and they will see themselves clearly with an all pervading love and confidence.

OBSERVATION BRINGS RELIEF

As you work with Impartial Self Observation, you will recognize yourself enjoying a new freedom from the negatives, the blocks, the limitations that kept you imprisoned and helpless on the roller coaster. With the passing of each day, you will notice changes happening in your life. Things will be calmer, and one day you'll realize that the roller coaster has stopped and you have stepped off.

You will start to see the world, yourself, and the people around you in a different light. Life will still have its ups and downs, but you will handle them better and start to enjoy life. You will realize that the True Self is within and without, and you have no need, no desire to identify with any negatives.

The difference between how you live with your True Self, may well bring negative reaction from people still living in the Conditioned or Mechanical Mind mode. There will be some who obstinately refuse to listen to anything you have learned. They will appear hurt and declare: "You're not the same person I used to know. You're different." They may even urge you to "see a counselor," or worse, "go see a doctor and get some anti-depressants." They want you back as the old predictable self with the Mechnical Mind. But you know the drill. Observe everything impartially.

JUDGING AS OPPOSED TO REACTION

Judging as we have seen is a mechanical response of the False Self. We live in an extremely judgmental society. People expect you to judge.

However, as you start to live with the True Self and find that the old face of judgment has dissolved, you may wonder how you will handle the differences between blacks, whites and greys, the differences between the positives and the negatives, and the rest.

The difference is that when you live with the True Self you have the ability, the light of consciousness, to see the necessity of choice judging without the urge to judge mechanically. There is no compulsion to judge, regardless of whether the subject is controversial and would normally trigger a conditioned response. You allow yourself now to judge in a state of knowing, a state of consciousness.

When you work in the light of the True Self, you will discover the ease of correct conscious judging. On the path however, there may be challenges. If you feel the False Self is creating illusions and that you are in fact being lured into Mechanical judging, always resort to Impartial Self Observation and learn from what happens.

The total benefits to be acquired from Impartial Self Observation may not be immediately evident, but they do manifest with the passing of time.

OVERCOMING THE FUTILITY OF GUILT

Alan G came to one of my True Self workshops. He brought with him a cloak of heavy guilt. As a regional sales director covering two Pacific coast states, he had been too busy to be with his children. "They grew up and I missed everything. I wasn't there for them," he said. "Now they're gone. So has my wife."

In order to remedy the situation he had spent time with his daughter and son. "I felt so guilty, I really went down. They said they wanted to see me, but they were being polite. I'm a failure as a father. Now I'm just depressed."

He started looking at his guilt and depression through Impartial Self Observation but it wasn't working. "I keep getting the feeling I'm supposed to be guilty," he said.

That's your Mechanical Mind. People with Conditioned Minds will all tell you: "You should feel guilty. It's part of human nature." Guilt, like anger, bitterness, jealousy and all the other many, many faces of the False Self do nothing for you, I told Alan. Guilt, like those other negative faces will undermine your health, and the worse thing is, it will do nothing positive for you.

Work at Impartial Self Obsrvation until you understand it, until the guilt and its associated faces of the False Self dissolve and never return. A couple of months later, Alan came into my office with great news. "Everything you taught me works! I've rented a large cottage on one of the Greek islands for six weeks. My wife and my kids are spending their summer holidays with me."

When you allow your Mechanical Mind to create a problem, you suffer pain, discomfort, embarrassment, depression, just a few of the faces of the Conditioned Mind. The problem multiplies. When you are bathed in the heavy darkness of guilt, like Alan, your pain, your guilt hurts others around you. They may try to help you, but as they are also living with Mechanical Minds with Conditioned responses, you and they won't get very far, and in the end, they will leave you.

Whatever happens in your life, particularly negative, mentally and physically unprofitable actions or feelings, always resort to

Impartial Self Observation. Done properly, it will allow you to break free from your cave and you will embrace the sunshine of the True Self. Paul's Glass Darkly will be but a memory.

JUDGE NOT LEST YE BE JUDGED

This is a very powerful piece of cosmic advice that has been handed down over the centuries, and yet many are obsessed with judging. We look in a mirror and judge ourselves. We also judge other people to the point of absurdity. This is when we judge others without possessing any real or valid knowledge of what of who we are judging.

A young woman was walking home in a suburban area. She decided to take a short-cut through a small park. There on what she thought was a secluded bench, was a couple of teenage lovers engaged in wild, passionate sex. Unable to believe her eyes, she stifled a shriek and ran home, totally disgusted. For weeks afterwards she told her family members and friends of the "vile, disgusting, depraved couple" and with each telling the narrative became more and more embellished.

As the months passed, the young woman met a man and fell deeply in love. One evening, after a romantic dinner, they went to bed – and suddenly the woman was gripped in fear and started screaming and sobbing. "It's vile, disgusting," she cried, "I can't do it." She never married and never engaged in sex which she always maintained was "vile and disgusting." Innocently, she had applied her judgment on another couple to herself. Judging is a double-edged sword.

RESIST LABELING

When we label something as good or bad, we automatically adopt the standard by which we have judged that something as good or bad. It is the same as success and failure. They are totally meaningless, but by believing these judgments we are forced to live with them.

The next time you wish to make a judgmental statement, put a label on someone or yourself, mentally switch on the video camera and watch yourself impartially. You will fnd it very difficult, if not impossible to make the statement. Allow this to happen every time you wish to do some labeling, and you will find the desire, the habit diminishing. And a strange sense of freedom sets in.

When you apply a negative judgment either to someone else or yourself, your emotional energy within contracts. It hardens. It becomes a burden and the False Self continues to reign. When you resist labeling and making judgments you will feel a cosmic freedom opening up in your life. Do not imagine what this freedom is like, allow yourself to be surprised and feel your energy expanding.

KILLING THE SUCCESS MONSTER

Success is an illusion. And yet millions of people are taught to strive for success. In schools, colleges, at home, young people are urged to excel and climb the ladder of success. There is nothing wrong in urging students to excel in their studies, in their achievements and ambitions. It is that strange and peculiar condition called success that Mechanical Society conditions the minds of young people growing up.

Get to the top of the success ladder, they are told. The truth eventually hits the ladder climbers. There's nothing at the top but an illusion. For some strange and stressful reason you feel you have to stay at the top of the ladder, because coming down means failure, and that's another illusion of the Mechanical Mind. Neither success nor failure exist outside of the Mechanical Mind.

Exile all thoughts, all conditioning about success and you will never ever suffer the feelings of failure. However always strive to do your personal best, simply resist comparing it to others. Remove the judgmental factor and enjoy your life.

SOME NOTES ON AWARENESS

As you work to dissolve the many faces of the False Self and the True Self starts to shine forth, you will start to observe that the world is full of suffering.

The mystic, the True Self philosopher does not accept that suffering. Work to see the suffering of the world and understand it. And if you start suffering too, perform Impartial Self Observation. Work to understand your suffering and observe what happens. Do not, under any circumstances deny that suffering does not exist. Suffering for many is a mechanical response.

It is similar to illness. The very word "illness" carries with it the stigma of possible death. Such words as illness and sickness trigger the imagination to build layers and layers of negativity within the mind. You only have to listen to the pharmaceutical advertisements that pepper our major television newscasts to understand how society – millions of people – are being subjected to alarm and despondency through "possible side effects" that include sicknesses far more serious and devastating than the condition the medicine is supposed to treat.

When you are exposed to such a commercial on television, do not walk away, change channels, or deny it, simply observe yourself, your reaction, your feelings. How does your body feel? How is your mind reacting? Observe everything without comment, etc. If there is a part of you that feels the world's suffering, observe your feelings.

People should be encouraged to think "health" not "sickness." Your body enjoys being told good, positive healthful suggestions, in fact it has been scientifically proven time and time again that the human body responds positively to prayer and healthy suggestions.

FREEING OURSELVES FROM ANXIETY

As you deal with the various faces of the negative ego, you may be aware of a whole lot of other faces of the False Self, and some may feel desperate. If it feels threatened the False Self will resort to all sorts of subversive and threatening strategies including manifesting restlessness and anxiety. Your job: observe them impartially as instructed before.

You may on occasions, feel as if you are having to deal with an armada, a whole flotilla of anxieties. Nil desperadum – never despair! An interesting phenomena will occur after several impartial observations. The armada, the fleet starts to sink. They slink away into the mists, and rarely will ever return, certainly not en masse. It's like a logger cutting down a critical tree in the forest, a whole lot of other trees start to topple.

Always be aware, the False Self's strength is based on memories, and memories are based on experiences such as pleasure, embarrassment, love, pain, jealousy, possession, and a host of similar patterns. All your limitations, fears and problems derive from such memories, and the greater the energy contained in a memory, the great impact it has with the False Self. When you strongly believe in these patterns, and they become repeatable through the Mechanical Mind, they will give the impression they cannot be changed, or they are needed for your security.

Habit makes these patterns permanent. They are illusions, as are all the faces of the False Self. Know that you can dissolve them and remove them from your life. The key is Self-Remembrance otherwise known as Impartial Self Observation.

BREAKING THE "I AM" TRAP

One part of the Mechanical Mind that will be brought into your field of awareness sooner or later, is the "I am" trap. It is a problem that stems from the False Self and it's called Identification.

With the creation of the False Self in our lives, we learn to identify. And the interesting thing is that our minds say them unconsciously without any regard to logic.

Be aware of the number of times in a day you make statements pre-fixed by the words "I am." I am a father. I am a mother. I am a shift-worker. I am a nurse. I am a Buddhist. I am black. I am married. And so the list goes on.

But then it starts to become complicated. I am an asthmatic. I am stupid. I am lazy. I am always late. I am a terrible lover. I am an arthritic. I am a sexual powerhouse. I am always sick. I am an insomniac. I am an alcoholic. I am jealous. I am angry.

When you state an "I am..." you are identifying with a particular condition. The problem really manifests itself is when you put a list together. If you observe yourself impartially during the course of the day, you will find you identify with many things. Hundreds of things, perhaps a thousand or more in just one day, depending on your interactions with others.

Apart from reaffirming considerable self-talk, you are identifying with a whole bunch of negatives. You are giving substance to conditions, which, if you really think about it, you wouldn't want to admit to yourself, let alone others.

However, if you practice Impartial Self Observation and watch yourself as you claim these well-used identifications, you may notice, as one identity dissolves under observation, many other negative identities or emotions you have not seen or thought about before start to manifest. You may wonder where they all come from. Practice Impartial Self Observation...and let them dissolve.

FEAR EXISTS IN THE IMAGINATION

The Old Testament Prophet, Job, said: "For the thing that I had greatly feared is come upon me..."

In today's language it is called negative imagery and it's a powerful tool of the Subconscious Mind and unless you are fully conscious of it, it can bring disastrous results in your life. Fear and anxiety are multi-faceted parts of the False Self. Fear is a total product of the imagination, and it exists based on memories of past events in your life, or past memories that feed the imagination for some future event.

Fear and anxiety provoke a stream of faces in the False Self, including anger, bitterness, worry, restlessness, revenge, isolation and thousands of other negative feelings and emotions. The very root of fear and anxiety is a lack of identity

As we mentioned earlier, Sigmund Freud once suggested that if it comes to a battle between reality and the imagination, the imagination will always win. The imagination used by the False Self can be destructive physically, mentally and spiritually.

Whenever a fear or an anxiety manifests in your life, watch it. Use your powers of Impartial Self Observation, without comment, criticism, judgment or opinion. Be totally detached. The fear may be over the loss of a special person in your life, the rejection of a job application, a scholarship or a bank loan. The fear may be over travelling on an aircraft, an escaltor, speaking to a group of people, or simply meeting new people.

I once knew a very nice lady who had a fear of being mugged. She took every precuation – which enhanced her fear – and eventually she was robbed. In hypnosis and utilizing self-observation she dissolved the fear and started living a better life.

Whatever your fear, know that it has no power over you. Observe everything as the fear or anxiety raises its old and ugly head. Observe where the fear is manifesting – in your head, chest, stomach, legs? Your skin? Your breathing? Where do you feel the pain, the discomfort? What is the fear doing to your body, your mind?

Under the powerful cosmic light of Impartial Self Observation you will find fear diminishes. As it dissolves maintain an impartial watch. Observe and let it go. As you practice these strategies, you will feel the positive power of the True Self starting to shine in your life, and you will now that you are doing the right thing.

KNOWING IS NOT THE SAME AS AWARENESS

"Knowledge is one thing, understanding is another thing." So said Gurdjieff. It's one of those confusing aspects, and many people fail to grasp the difference between them. "Understanding depends upon the relation of knowledge to being," he said.

Knowledge by itself does not provide understanding, nor is understanding increased by the accumulation of more knowledge. Many people, still thinking mechanically, fail to grasp the significance, and continue to accumulate knowledge without attaining understanding.

In order to understand, one must experience knowledge. It must be felt at all levels of your being, and this is called awareness. If knowledge outweighs being, and a person does not make it part of being, it is simply useless knowledge.

For instance, many people flock to hear great speakers in seminars and workshops, and they accumulate much knowledge on metaphsyics, cosmic awareness, healing, spirituality. While they return home with considerable amounts of new knowledge, they don't understand what they have stored, because to understand requires that knowledge must be felt, not just by the mind, but by one's entire existence – body, mind and spirit. Failure to understand results from the mechanical mind, the conditioned mind. The False Self blocks the ability to understand and live fully.

What are these blocks? They can be thought of as walls – walls of the mind. They prevent one from experiencing knowledge and thus understanding knowledge. You might claim you are unaware of such walls. That is exactly why. Because you are unaware, you cannot tear them down. You cannot remove them. When you encounter such walls, such blocks, be aware of them, do not fight them, simply observe impartially and allow them to dissolve.

HOW TO ACHIEVE TRUE HAPPINESS

One of the most misunderstood faces of the negative ego is unhappiness. People the whole world over are desperately seeking happiness. Most people find happiness and then, much to their concern it fades. Happiness for them is like a meteorite, a shooting star. It burns brightly for a short period, then it is gone.

When I conducted spiritual awareness classes in Vancouver, a middle aged, well dressed man would occasionally sit in our circle.

We learned he was obsessed with winning the lottery—big time. "I shall never be really happy until I can walk into the lottery commission's office and say - pay me!" he said. Some twenty years later, I met him on the SkyTrain rapid transit system. "No, I' m still waiting. It'll happen." He grinned and walked on. The last I heard, he was still banking his happiness on a major lottery win.

There is a truth that has been handed down by the ancients. It is this:

All unhappiness results from wanting something that you cannot have. There are no exceptions.

Let us review some examples: You want your teenage son to stop being friendly with "those kids across the tracks." He ignores you. The person you thought was your "soul mate" has gone off with another and you smoulder wanting that person to come back. Examples range through every aspect of life, and in all cases, you will realize that you are creating your own unhappiness by wanting something you cannot have.

You might be more worldly in your unachievable wants. I want the world to stop fighting. I want all wars to end. I want killing to stop. I want every person in the world to live in a state of love. While these may be very admirable desires, if wanting them makes you unhappy, you have fallen into the suffering trap.

Whenever you encounter a situation in which you find you are blocked and unhappiness results, use your imagined video camera technique: watch yourself completely with impartial self-observation. Work to understand where this damaging face of the negative ego is coming from. Be fully aware and allow the unhappiness to dissolve, and an interesting phenomenon occurs - you receive a glimpse, a flash of happiness.

This is similar to the other human condition: You cannot be stressed and relaxed at the same time.

You cannot feel unhappy and be happy. Likewise, you cannot feel relaxed and stressed at the same time. We are not talking about the temporary happiness, the shooting star happiness. There's no comparison. This is the happiness that transcends all imagination. It is a lasting phenomenon. You might call it an eternal happiness, a cosmic happiness, a mystic happiness. It is a pure, ineffable state of being, a state of consciousness which defies description, and does not depend on anything out there. It is close and you can reach it.

REMEMBERING YOURSELF

One of the old Sufi philosophers, Sheikh Ismail Hakki put it this way: *Everything is dependent upon remembering. One does not begin by learning, one starts by remembrance. The distance of eternal existence and the difficulties of life cause one to forget. It is for this reason God commanded us: "Remember!"*

If you ask anyone: Can you remember yourself? They will probably offer the comment that they can recall events in their life back to the age of five or six, perhaps even three or four. As we mentioned earlier, the sub-conscious mind can recall many events that extend well beyond a person's conscious ability. The day you first walked: who was there, what you were wearing, what people said. But when we say "Remember yourself" we are talking about being able to stay and focus on your True Self. To be you, totally and without question.

Near the beginning of this book, you may recall I asked you to put the book down and be aware. That was a glimpse of the aim of this book. It would be inconsiderate if I said awareness is easy to achieve. With perseverance and desire, it can be done. Normally, total awareness will come in small flashes, and gradually as you progress, the flashes will be prolonged and eventually lead to a life of True Self awareness.

You might be very proud of your mental prowess but the truth is the False Self can only focus on one point at a time. For instance, consider Cause and Effect, which is also known as Karma. It is impossible to think of the Cause of a situation, and the Effect at the same time. Our mechanical minds cannot deal with both at the same time because the False Self will view each as a separate entity.

The mechanical mind does not allow a person to be conscious of himself or herself. For instance, recall when you were talking to other people regarding a project, buying a car, arranging a vacation, students doing their homework, or simply discussing the news of the day. Where was your consciousness?

If you look back, you will recall expressing yourself with such statements as "I think..." or "I dislike..." or "I like..." or "I'm not sure," but were you conscious at the time? During these activities in which you participated, a number of different faces of the ego were displayed. But did they reveal the True Self, or did they in reality display the old mechanical self and its set of programmed responses? As we have seen there are many different "I"s, different faces in the False Self.

We are dealing with Self Consciousness. This is not the situation where you are suddenly embarrassed by an event and turn red-faced, this is the self consciousness that you experience when you are doing and saying all the examples we mentioned in the previous paragraph. It is self-remembering.

When you place the False Self under your own mental microscope it is a fast and complete method for self-remembering. The more you watch the False Self, the more you remember yourself, the more you become one with the True Self.

The False Self will attempt to prevent you from self-remembering. It has no desire for self-remembrance, in fact it will attempt to block any moves you make to remember yourself. The False Self demands to be in charge. It is only happy when it is flashing the many faces of the negative ego.

Work to understand the False Self, practice impartial self observation at every opportunity and you will find the False Self losing its grip and becoming weaker and weaker as the days progress. Some mechanically minded people may suggest that the False Self will become less effective and leave you naturally as you become older. The opposite is true. The False Self actually becomes stronger and more evident as one gets older. Observe many older people.

Exercise: Get Special Help

An interesting exercise that works very well is this: The next time you find yourself in a heated debate and you find yourself saying all the wrong things that seem to stoke more ire among people around you, decide to pause, and go into your Inner Mind. You need help. Of all the great teachers, review from whom you would appreciate help: Moses, Jesus, Mohammed, Buddha, Plotinus, Solomon, Homer, Robert Browning, Walt Whitman and so on.

Next, silently pray to whoever you pray to, and ask that one of these great teachers and mystics, could help and show you the way. You could say: *"This discussion is not going the right way, and it's becoming very negative. Please take over my body. I will stand aside to watch and learn. Amen."* Then take a slow deep breath and as you breathe out feel the energy in your body and mind change. You will still be you, but you will see, hear and feel things differently. People in the group may express surprise and even be pleasantly stunned by the change of the wisdom that flows from your body.

Afterwards, find yourself a quiet place where you will not be disturbed, say a prayer of thanks and mull over the energy and the feelings that you have learned.

When the False Self starts to fade, starts to lose its power and seems to slip away into the night, you will discover the same energy, the same feelings that you experienced when you asked for help from higher powers.

You will find as these feelings and energies stay with you, you will have an understanding, a wisdom and a great feeling of Self no matter what you do, and no matter where you go, and whoever you are with. The True Self will give you a new consciousness in which you will find a deep, inner sense of life. The Universe will appear differently and be beautiful beyond description. You will also feel a close relationship to the Creator, the Source of Your Being. God.

"Let nothing trouble you, let nothing frighten you. All things are passing; God never changes." St. Teresa of Avila followed the mystical teachings and was harassed by higher authority in the church for many years.

DO YOU RECOGNIZE THE TRUE SELF?

If you haven't recognized it yet, this is the time when you come face to face with that Elusive True Self.

Think about this. When you are watching the various faces of the False Self; the comings and goings of different thoughts, the various feelings and emotions that come and go, when you practice Impartial Self Observation, consider the process. What is producing the faces of the False Ego? What is maintaining the Mechanical Mind? What is projecting the stream of thoughts?

It's the Sub-conscious Mind, and that we will call the Thinker. So, if the Sub-conscious Mind is the Thinker, who is doing the watching? Who is the quiet observer? Who is watching those thoughts coming and going without identifying with those many faces of the False Self ? Who has the power to stay detached and observe the Mechanical Mind impartially?

Welcome to the world of your True Self.

It is that part of you that is able to detach itself from the fields of the mechanical mind, the conditioned mind. It has the power to say, "I can watch my mental processes. I do not need to get involved. I simply maintain my role as a watcher, an observer. I do not need to make judgments, cast opinions, because I am free. I am simply here to learn."

This is what Jesus the Teacher of Gallilee was teaching in the Sermon on the Mount. The problem was, the teachings were so far up the mystical scale that only a few carried the vital message. Most Christians, including many priests, have no idea of the mystical teachings of Jesus, and so in their emptiness, they created strange symbolism and intimidating dogmas to cover their ignorance and keep the faithful in the cave.

As you progress with your exercises and embrace your True Self, you will realize that you have broken free from the prison, the cave of the Mechanical Mind. Paul's Glass Darkly is gone. You may realize that you are leaving many loved ones, friends, colleagues and others behind, and you may feel an urge to rush to their side and joyfully announce what you have discovered.

Your Higher Self, your True Self may whisper caution. Be careful. The joyful urge can be self-sabotage. It may be coming from the old self, the Mechanical Mind, attempting to undermine your new found freedom. The urge may well be another of the faces of the False Self, and if you go along with it, you may find yourself severely rejected by the loved ones you are trying to help. In other words, you may well get shunned, stoned and even crucified. If they feel considerate, they may even cry: "Come down here and be normal (miserable) like us."

It's happened to many learned folk throughout the ages who found a fast, one way trip into the Book of Martyrs. Martyrs serve no useful purpose, except to entertain the people who are doing the martyring. Jesus the Teacher told us not to throw pearls before swine. But he failed to listen to his own teachings and the crucifiers got him. Jesus only taught for three years. Think how much richer the world would be if he had walked the Earth for forty or fifty years teaching the people.

As you walk and live with your True Self, you are a pilgrim on the Mystic Path. There is some sound advice among mystics: "Never promote the teachings. Allow a student to ask a question and only reply to the question." If you follow this aged-old advice, you will find your newly found consciousness is safe and sound.

Before we leave this section, I would like to point out there is an excellent example of someone dealing with his own False Self. After being baptized, Jesus the Nazarene fasted for forty days and nights in the desert. It was during this time that the Devil otherwise known as the False Self tempted him with power and promises but the Teacher persistently rejected these advances. Afterwards Angels came and brought nourishment. Descriptions are found in the texts of Matthew, Mark and Luke. Interestingly, it is also found in the ancient

Aramaic Matthew. Theologians frequently refer to the False Self as the "Devil within."

THE QUIET MIND

As you practice Self Remembering, dissolving the Negative Ego and Mechanical Thinking you will probably come across a disconcerting phenomenon known as "No think" or "Not Knowing." Ever since the Aryan mystics developed the process, no-think has been the foundation of Being, the basis of taking one beyond thought.

Various surveys indicate some 47 million Americans are not having enough sleeps mainly because of "mind chatter." Their thoughts triggered by anger, stress, anxiety – all faces of the False Self – are out of control resulting in various health problems. One wonders why when the ancient teachings are openly available.

For many in modern day society, the idea of no-think, the concept of not knowing can be disconcerting, even terrifying. If the idea of no-think creates anxiety go back and subject it to Impartial Self Observation. Once you have achieved the state of no-think and feel comfortable you can understand that you have gone beyond the Mechanical Mind into the outer realms of what Richard Bucke called "Cosmic Consciousness."

At first, the state of no-think will endure for perhaps a few seconds, but it will be as if a door, a gateway has been opened and you will desire to return. Practice understanding your False Self and observe it diminishing, and feel the growing presence of your True Self.

If you have found the first part of this book life-changing, the second part will offer you the time of your life.

FOR NOW POINTS TO REMEMBER

- o Many things in these mystical teachings are complete reversals of what you have been trained to think.
- o You have the power to dissolve dangerous illusions.

o To discover your own True Self you need to have the desire and passion to do nothing, except observe and learn.

o Resist judging and you will be free.

o Nothing is what it seems because you have the power to change the way you see it.

o Whatever you do in your life, love yourself for doing it and you will always do the right thing.

o Never make imaginative assumptions as to the nature of your Higher Self, your True Self.

o The Mechanical Mind, the Conditioned Mind is an illusion, but because you believe it exists, you live with it.

o The False Self cannot be controlled or suppressed, but by shining the Light of Awareness, the faces start to dissolve.

o Impartial Self Observation is the entrance, the pathway, the Gateway to a new sense of Self, the True Self.

o Impartial Self Observation should always be conducted without comment, criticism, judgment, and an expression of opinion or feelings.

o Knowledge by itself does not provide understanding, nor is understanding increased by the accumulation of more knowledge.

o All unhappiness results from wanting something that you cannot have. There are no exceptions. You can achieve lasting happiness.

o Success and failure are dangerous illusions. Eliminate conditioned beliefs about success and you will never suffer failure.

2

BEYOND THE MIND.
LIVING IN THE HERE AND NOW

"We are here and now living in Infinity and Eternity."
  – W.J. Colville, British medium and author.

OBSERVING THE THINKER

Simply close your eyes for a few moments and watch, mentally observe your mind thinking. What is your mind thinking about. Spend a minute or so just observing your mind think. Resist getting involved with the thoughts, just observe.

Now, who is doing the thinking? Is it the physical person which you may perhaps identify as your body? Is it the mental person with which you may perhaps identify your brain?

So, if we have one part of you thinking, and another part of you watching, being the observer, we have separation. We have something, a quality, an entity that is able to watch your body and mind thinking.

Therefore, if you can watch your own thought processes, that mechanical mind generating thoughts, who is doing the watching, the observing?

Welcome to the True Self. As you progress you will realize that your thoughts are not you, and you are not your thoughts.

One thing more. While you were doing this exercise did you realize you were living in the Here and Now?

LEARNING TO LIVE IN THE NOW

When you rush headlong from one moment to another, wondering if you're going to be on time for work, an appointment, anticipating a road block, feeling desperate for being with the person or people important in your life, you have missed something incredibly beautiful, something that cannot be repeated. You have missed the ecstasy of the Here and Now, and you are still on the roller coaster.

Imagine you are in a movie theater and they are showing a film of your life. See yourself sitting in the front row – Now! – watching the passing tapestry, the kaleidoscope of memories of your life But you are not really watching it. Chances are you are thinking about all the things that the film has recounted in your life. You start to feel guilty, ashamed, embarrassed over a lot of things. You regret missing an opportunity to get a great career, meet a special person, having a time with someone who has now gone.

Your good memories of the past hurt because they didn't last. What if it could happen again. You start thinking of the film to come. You dwell on making the same mistakes. "Maybe I'll get sick, maybe I won't have a pension before the movie of my life ends." You start to fear the future. You have lost the joy of living in the Here and Now, the wonder of living in the present. Like millions of people, you are condemned to either live in the past or dwell on the future.

Difficult to believe? Prove it to yourself. Simply listen to people talking: perhaps members of your family, or while you are sitting in a busy café or surrounded by people at work. No matter where you go, people will be living in the past or the future. For many people, the present, the Here and Now does not exist.

You might argue, "I know I'm here. I know I am reading your book. I'm quite conscious of where I am. I'm always conscious, why only yesterday I was discussing meditation..."

I interrupt. "For a brief moment you were in the present. The moment you slipped into a past memory – only yesterday – you forgot yourself. You were in another day, another time, and with another person."

As George Gurdjieff said: "Your principal mistake consists in thinking that you always have consciousness, and in general, either that consciousness is always present or that it is never present."

Consciousness is very difficult, if not impossible to define, which is why many people, including scientists and philosophers fail to set any qualities or quantities because they are virtually impossible to nail down. However, you can enjoy flashes of Here and Now consciousness, and here once again, your experience cannot be defined in words.

Back to the movie being shown. You are not concerned with what has past. You remember it but it does not bother you. You have no concerns about the movie scenes to come, you simply focus on the present – you watch the screen and live in the Here and Now.

When you learn to live your life as it is happening now, you live in sublime ecstasy. Your life is free from the hurts of the past and the fears of the future. You can be involved in a hectic, apparent frenzied scramble at work or play and be entirely centered in the Here and Now.

The Yogis have a very interesting observation when they ask: "If you are not enjoying yourself right now, when will you enjoy yourself?"

Exercise: Observing The Here And Now

After you have read this exercise, keep holding this book, take a deep breath, and as you breathe out, be conscious of where you are; Observe how you are positioned. Sense your body. Note how is it feeling? Resist judging or even commenting on it. Sense or mentally watch your body breathing in and breathing out. Observe your clothes on your skin. Be conscious of your own presence, your own existence.

Then, when you are ready, read this paragraph again and as you do, sense your body, sense your environment as you are reading the words. Observe how your eyes are working as you read these words. Feel or sense the presence of yourself. You may notice that you are watching yourself. This is enlightened consciousness. When you have completed this exercise, review the feeling of peace that enveloped you as you did it. You may have felt it was a cocoon or an aura of peace. This is what Gurdjieff called self-remembering.

You can also experience the Here and Now by performing the following: take a potato or an orange, and standing outside where there is plenty of room, decide to toss the object in the air–10 or 20 feet–and as you watch it come down, decide to catch it with both hands. Feel the object leave your hands, watch it passing through the air, and then observe as it comes back into your hands.

Immediately afterwards, think about the action. Where were your thoughts? Where was your concentration? Chances are, they were on the action. They were neither in the past nor the future. You were living in the Here and Now.

With practice you can live in the Here and Now. It will make a startling difference to your life, because the quiet sense of consciousness feels like a breath of fresh air, a sense of ecstasy, a sense of Being. Freedom!

When you are living in the Here and Now, you do not concern or even worry yourself about tomorrow's activities, tomorrow's enjoyment. Throughout our lives our mechanical minds have been trained to live, to dwell, either in the future or the past. It's almost as if our ancestors did not want us to recognize Here and Now living.

PRACTICE, PRACTICE, PRACTICE

As my old friend and colleague Tom Passey, one of Canada's top dowsers used to say: "Anything that demands development in metaphysics, higher awareness and spiritual enhancement demands practice." He would drill it into our students: "Practice! Practice! Practice."

If you desire to be a good skier, a good concert pianist, a ballet dancer, a good swimmer, a mountain climber, a good tennis player or golfer, you need to be committed to practice. It's interesting that I mentioned these activities because when they are performed properly you cannot be anywhere else than in the Here and Now. You are pulled into self-remembering. If you are downhill skiing on a black diamond, and your consciousness drifts away onto some domestic or relationship problem, the moment that drift happens, you're in a potential disaster zone where accidents happen. You're out of the Here and Now.

For some time, until you have mastered the process, you will find yourself breaking away into the past or future. Observe yourself impartially, and immediately pull yourself back into the Here and Now. Do not feel guilty, or even suggest you are a failure – that's the old False Self raising its head. Just bring your consciousness back to self-remembering and resume the joy of living in the Here and Now.

PASSION FUELS YOUR GOAL

Besides practice, another quality required for living in the here and now is passion and desire. This is a prerequisite for achieving any goal or objective in your life. Passion is the fire, the burning desire to achieve something. It is no use doing anything in higher awareness to please someone else – your partner in life, a friend or simply to prove to yourself that it cannot be done. You need to be able to say: "There has to be something better than the hypnotic sleep state. I am achieving my mission. I am escaping." Always use the present tense when creating self-talk. As I will explain in a couple of pages, the subconscious mind, the mechanical mind does not recognize the future. Words such as "try" and "can" have no meaning for the Inner Mind.

Now, as you practice these things, particularly living in the Here and Now, and applying impartial self-observation, you will find that your world is changing. As you practice you'll receive glimpses of your new world, and there maybe days when you fail to get any glimpses at all. Persevere and always you will be amply rewarded.

As you walk and truly live in the Here and Now, you will find that you can still look at the future and the past, but you will no longer identify with them. As I have told many a client, "Learn from the past, plan for the future, but live in the Here and Now."

When you live in the present, you will see the future clearly, unclouded by dusty shrouds of fears, doubts and limitations. Your intuitive powers will excel and you will benefit. The past will be a series of memories, much like a box of very old movies which no longer entertain you.

It will be like having a book, that having once reviewed, you snap close the hard covers and replace it on the shelf. However, because you are living in the Here and Now, you will always have the choice of opening the book and reading its content. You will be the master, and not a slave on a roller coaster.

Exercise: Walking In The Here And Now

When you are walking in the open air, mentally observe how your body is moving. What are the physical sensations, how are your feet feeling as they touch the ground. Do you feel heavy? Light? Sluggish? Is the sun shining? How does it feel on your body? Observe how your body is breathing? Is there increased breathing since you started walking? Perform some or all of these functions and do it completely without judgment, criticism, or comment. Notice how you feel when you finish walking – again without judgment. Be totally impartial.

YOUR SUBCONSCIOUS IS POWERFUL, BUT...

Your subconscious mind is an extremely powerful faculty. Scientists have been struggling with the human subconscious to find out exactly where it is located and how it operates. The average brain consists of about one hundred billion neurons, which might be an impressive number, but the real power and complexity of the brain comes through its connections. Scientists believe that "every aspect of consciousness can be tied to the brain," wrote Steven Pinker, Professor of Psychology at Harvard, a statement that riled many spiritualists and metaphysical people because at death, he claimed "the person's consciousness goes out of existence."

As we mentioned earlier, the subconscious mind has an enormous power for remembering. Based on the power of emotions, it stores data from your life, and retrieves such data easily and effortlessly within a fraction of a second. Observe yourself. It happens without warning.

You're walking along and you spot someone coming towards you. Flash! Your sub-conscious in a split second suddenly reminds you of someone who was in your distant past. It may have been twenty, thirty, forty years ago, but your subconscious mind has the ability to match what you are seeing as you walk along, with a face tucked away in your memory banks—and you didn't know that memory even existed. But it all happened, seemingly at the speed of light. That is a demonstration of the power of the subconscious.

While the subconscious mind is a powerhouse of the past and the present it has no concept of the future.

Exercise: 'I Can" Or "I Am"?

Dr. Al Krasner, a great teacher of Hypnotherapy taught me this exercise and I use it frequently to explain the logic of the subconscious mind.

Find yourself a pencil or a pen and hold it between your thumb and first finger. Allow your finger and thumb to flick it back and forth. Then focus intently on the pencil and say out loud: **"I can drop it. I can drop it. I can drop it."** Say this repeatedly with no interruption. Keep focused and see if you can drop the pen or pencil from your fingers, and you will find the harder you try, the tighter your grip becomes on the pencil.

Then suddenly change your voice and say: **"I am dropping it."** If you have done the exercise correctly, the grip in your fingers will be gone instantly, almost before you have finished saying it, and the pen or pencil will slip out of your fingers.

Performed properly, you have just discovered a very interesting phenomenon within your subconscious mind. The powerhouse that collects and stores countless bygone memories and records everything happening within and around you now, does not recognize the future. It has no concept of the future. The only future it can conceive is based on memories and they are all illusions. They do not exist.

Why? When you say "I can" that, to the subconscious mind is ambiguous. It is somewhere in the future and it does not understand that. Then when you said "I am" that is now, this instant and the subconscious mind responds.

This is why if you say: I will try and lose weight," or "I can quit smoking" among other objectives, you will never achieve them. Tell yourself repeatedly: "I am a non-smoker" or "I am losing weight," and your subconscious mind instantly takes notice.

It knows of no other time. This is the validator. Future time is an illusion, but by believing it exists, you lose much of the beauty of living in the Here and Now. When you see and live with the truth, you find your life suddenly becomes priceless.

THE PHENOMENA CALLED TIME

Something you may wish to consider is the fact that everything you think is in the Here and Now, you cannot think in the past. But you would be surprised at how many people identify with events that happened long ago. Most people are too busy living in an illusion of time, living in the future or the past. Time past and time future do not exist in reality. There is only one time and that is Now. But don't fall for it: this too is an illusion.

Now is an illusion because the moment you are conscious of it, it has gone. It's history. It's like that film running through the projector. The picture you see in an instant is already in the past. Time is constantly moving – at least that is the image. For instance, you cannot grab it, stop it, even prevent it as it apparently hurtles through your life.

This may come as a surprise, but you can only measure time as the illusion passes through. You cannot measure time that supposed-ly happened half an hour ago, or even yesterday. You wouldn't want to think of measuring time tomorrow. You can only measure it while it is passing through your life, your consciousness. A clock only keeps pace of so called time because astronomers figured out, long ago, that this would be a useful thing for society.

Yesterday is gone. You cannot change anything that happened yesterday – only the way you see it. And when you do reflect on a memory, that reflection is always in the present. Tomorrow never comes because simply it is always tomorrow. What does come, and it is here as you read this, is today. But even as you read this sentence, the action is already in the past. Time is a slippery little thing.

When you speak to another person, your vocal sounds are already in the past. When you watch sports on television, they may flash "live" on the screen, but in effect, when you see it, it is already in the past.

The only way you can live in the Here and Now is to consciously decide that you are doing it. And do it. Learn to appreciate time, but know that you are appreciating an illusion.

Among the ancient teachers and philosophers who featured the Here and Now in their works was the multi-talented Leonardo da Vinci.

Exercise: Leonardo Da Vinci's River

In his famous Notebooks Leonardo noted that if you dip your hand in a river, *you are touching the last of all that has past and the beginning of that which is to come.* Profound words. Think about them. As you read these words, you are living the last of all that is past in your life, and the first of that which is to come.

Relax in meditation, and see yourself sitting by Leonardo's river and imagine you are dipping your hand into the beautiful water. Focus on your hand, and recall da Vinci's words. Focus on the meditation and the words and you will find yourself experiencing living in the Here and Now. Be aware of your hand in the water. Be conscious of the water flowing through and round your fingers? Is it cold or warm? Note the pressure of the current on your hand. How do you feel as you envisage touching the water? Afterwards, observe how your body and mind were feeling while you performed the meditation. You may be pleasantly surprised.

AUGUSTINE KNEW THIS VITAL TRUTH

Catch onto this important truth. There is only one time and that is Here and Now. One of the ancient teachers who studied time intensely was St. Augustine of Hippo who lived from 354 – 430 AD. He shared his thoughts with God in his famous "Confessions." First of all, he discovered that when we use words to describe time we are "generally inaccurate and seldom completely correct, but our meaning is recognized none the less." He suggested that it is not strictly correct to say there are three times, past, present and future.

Augustine explains it like this. The present of past things is memory, and the memory is experienced NOW. The present of future things is expectation, but those expectations are experienced NOW. The present of present things is direct perception – which is NOW. In other words, all our thinking, awareness, self-consciousness, self remembrance takes place NOW. It cannot be otherwise.

Augustine told God that time does not exist. It cannot be measured in the past and it cannot be measured in the future. It can only be measured as it passes through, much like the analogy of the train we gave earlier.

To confuse things even further, the present time – Now – has no duration, so it cannot be measured, and it really is not time.

Augustine wrote on time: "...it is coming out of what does not yet exist, passing through what has no duration, and moving into what no longer exists." In other words, we all live in the Here and Now, and the sooner we remember ourselves and recognize that it is our choice, the sooner we will discover that peace that lies within, or as Jesus the teacher said: "Behold, the Kingdom of God is within you."

Eric Butterworth, the Unity Minister described heaven this way. "It is not a place in space but an inner potentiality of imprisoned splendor which is released through you. Thus the windows of heaven are in you. The windows of heaven are you!"

It may be difficult for someone coming out of the Mechanical, Conditioned Mind process of living to even imagine that a person can attain a total, ecstatic peace found only in the Here and Now while sitting amid the hordes hell-bent for the material meccas of New York, Los Angeles, Paris, Tokyo and London on the morning trains. But it happens.

I mentioned earlier in this book spirits of loved ones coming through to people in the physical frequently demonstrate the non-existence of the negative ego, or a greatly reduced ego. The Mechanical Mind disappears when one dies. Also entities in the Spirit World have little conception of time, simply because in the spirit world all entities live in the Here and Now.

THE ATTRACTION OF HERE AND NOW

Living in the Here and Now has been described as waking up, living with your eyes open. Some people claim that the ultimate ecstasy is meditation, which is closing your eyes and retreating. Living in the Now allows one to keep the eyes wide open and observe the wonders of the world and life.

Living in the Here and Now, without the hindrance of memory or the fears of the future, allows one to see and experience everything in a new light. Why? Because you see and appreciate everything in a new and unbiased way. You witness a sunrise, view a blooming rose, or greet an old friend in a fresh way. You enjoy being in the Here and Now without the drag of yesterday.

Memories distort our visions and perceptions. They impose limitations on our thinking and actions. Memories have no place in the Here and Now because as Scott Shaw so aptly puts it: "Memories lie. The Now cannot lie."

These points have many ramifications, as we shall see. One of these is opinions and judgments. Many a person has been killed because opinions conflict, and so too, many a country has gone to war because of one person's opinion. If you are practicing Impartial Self Observation on your opinions and judgments, you will already know how opinions, like a mist, can dissipate in the winds of true knowledge. Leonardo noted: "The greatest deception men suffer is from their own opinions." He added that many have made a trade of delusions and false miracles, "deceiving the stupid multitude."

Another advantage of living in the Here and Now is one cannot be depressed, feel pain or fear, be lonely, frustrated, unloved, angry, jealous and much more. If you think about it, all of these conflicts reside in memory and manifest in the faces of the False Self, and as we have seen, memories have no place in the Here and Now. Understand that fear, an emotion based upon something that might happen, has its seeds and fuel in past memories.

As you start to live in the Here and Now, you will find yourself being more worldly, more assertive, more in control. You will do things for the right reasons and not the old ones stemming from the Mechanical Mind. You will find the True Self, the Higher Self, emerging in your life, and you will be at one with it.

SLOWING DOWN YOUR TIME

If you have ever thought that there is not enough time in your day, that hours, days and weeks seem to pass with staggering rapidity. Birthdays come and go with a peculiar rapidity. You may also recall that when you were young, the days used to drag. Summer vacations seemed endless. Now they pass helter-skelter and you may frequently declare "There is not enough time in the day."

The problem is perception and it is embedded in your consciousness. The False Self is totally preoccupied with either the past or the future. It will play havoc with your life creating emotional upheavals such as fears of being late, the insecurity of missing an appointment, the idea that you will not have enough time to conduct your agenda. All these fears are based on past memories upon which the False Self projects your future.

The False Self for many people is their own worst enemy. It's like having a personal terrorist working in the corridors of your mind. It will hound and harass you, and if there is a history of mental imbalance, drive you to self-destruction.

The False Self has no concept of the Here and Now. It may get you to say that it understands the Here and Now very well, but that again is blatantly false. It may suggest you add more time to your day, but this is psychological time, it is a hopeless illusion.

There is only one way to release yourself from the dilemma of time, and that is to remove time from your consciousness. When you do this, you eliminate in one stroke, the False Self. It cannot exist without time.

This is not to say you eliminate time from your external life, your external agenda. Time is the currency on which the world maintains organization and balance. You need to keep appointments, get to work on time, take the kids to a ball game on time. The time we are discussing is the internal time, the time maintained by the False Self. It is time based on countless past memories that fuels the fears of future demands.

Observe your reaction to the False Self and its portrayal of time. When you use Impartial Self- Observation on time presented by the False Self, you will see clearly, that you are being deceived, hurt, and manipulated by the Negative Ego. Watch it without comment, without judgment, without criticism on each occasion as it attempts to harass and hurt you, and you will find the False Self and its use of time fading away. Eventually, that psychological time will no longer bother you and you will be free.

THE TYRANNY OF WAITING

For many years I worked in broadcast news and newspaper journalism where one has to work to the clock – the inevitable deadlines. One's whole structure, subsequently becomes used to the ticking clock. People whose lives depend on time, such as stockbrokers, transit workers, shift workers, and many others unwittingly become slaves to the dreaded mantra: Time is money.

Even when you change careers to a more relaxed environment, the clock still bothers one. A friend is not on time for a luncheon date, someone is late for picking up your child to go to school, the store is not opening on time, the doctor is running an hour late at the clinic. There are many instances of things not happening on time, and if you're a slave to time, it can really bother you.

Seriously consider these words: there is nothing, absolutely nothing which you need to wait for. Your False Self, your Conditioned Mind will quickly tell you that waiting is a waste of your precious time. The faces of the Negative Ego flash across your consciousness: Nervousness, irritation, frustration, anger, indignation and more.

Break free! You have the power. Observe these feelings impartially, then simply remember yourself. Bring your focus into the Here and Now. Whatever you are doing, bring yourself into the now where there is no pressure, no stress, and you know you are in the right place. This does not mean that you will never have to wait for anyone ever again, far from it.

Remember the next time you have to wait to see a doctor, meet a friend or a colleague for lunch, remember yourself, focus on yourself, be totally in the Here and Now. First mentally observe your breathing, then how your body is standing or sitting. Notice your posture. How are your clothes feeling on your body? Your shoes. How are they positioned? Then broaden your vision. Notice your environment. Watch the people moving by you. Observe their movements. Observe their faces. Observe how you are reacting to what you are observing. If there are trees, flowers or plants around, observe them. If a thought comes up that disturbs your observations, observe it - impartially - and watch it fade away.

When you use a time of waiting to remember yourself, and live in the Here and Now, you will find an incredible peace. You will enjoy the freshness, the total solitude. Your body and mind will slip into a beautiful aura of relaxation and freedom.

YOU HAVE MISSED NOTHING

Many a client has walked into my office and complained about their life. "I have had so many opportunities for success but I've missed every one. I think I'm a failure. Help me to find another opportunity."

First of all "success" and "failure" are faces of the False Self, the Conditioned Mind. They are illusions based on memories. In reality they have no existence, but because you believe in them, you feel they are real.

To achieve "success" or "failure" you have always compared yourself to others. Somewhere along the highway of life, someone taught you how to compare yourself to others, either deliberately or by example. Basic educational schools falsely teach this in the futile hope that you will advance in your learnings. Parents or relatives may well have added to this pressure. All this was conditioning in times past and the problem is hurting you, causing suffering now.

There is only one person in the whole wide world who is responsible for you, and that is you. You have the ability to achieve anything you want to achieve. Believe in yourself. Resist comparing yourself to others. Let no one talk you out of anything you wish to achieve. Observe impartially how others speak to you, and you will discover they speak from the False Self, the Mechanical Mind.

Focus on living in the Here and Now. Image yourself achieving whatever the goals are in your life. When you meditate or perform self-hypnosis, envision yourself achieving your goal. See yourself achieving it Now. Don't make the mistake of visualizing it in the future--that's another trap of the Conditioned Mind. Live, think, envision your goal in the Here and Now.

This is nothing new. The great teachers have been telling us for years to image in the now. For instance, Jesus the Teacher said: "Therefore I tell you, whatever you ask in prayer, believe that you have received it, and it will be yours."

Believe that you have received it! Not next week, not next year, but now, Right now! Prayer is a supplication to the Cosmos, your Creator, the Source of your Being. If you need something to improve your life - a companion, a home of your own, a car, a degree, a holiday, improved health, go into meditation and envision yourself living in that home, see yourself driving that car, envision yourself with improved health. Make your visions real. See them in bright colors. Color is energy.

Jesus the Gallilean also taught this other powerful mystical message: "Ask and you shall receive." It's simple. Incredibly simple. Ask and you shall receive. You have to ask to receive something. But you would be surprised at how many people, unhappy victims of their Mechanical Minds will say, "Oh, I'm not worthy... I'm unlucky...I don't deserve these things...I will always be poor."

Your Mechanical Mind creates limitations based on past memories, past teachings, past experiences. It's keeping you in your cave. Observe all these things, impartially as you live in the Here and Now.

And if you hear a little voice echoing skepticism, observe it impartially, because the False Self can be truly sneaky. It detests and fights anything new, as you may have discovered if you have been practicing the exercises in this book.

MIND CHATTER PAST AND FUTURE

Have you ever had trouble getting to sleep, or when you are asleep, you wake up and start that dreaded trend of thinking? That terrible mind chatter that simply will not go away.

Well, you're not alone. According to the National Sleep Foundation polls dating back to 1999, over half of America's adults experience one or more symptoms of insomnia at least a few nights a week. In the polls an amazing 32 per cent woke up often during the night, 38 per cent woke up in the morning feeling unrefreshed and 21 per cent wake up early.

When I question clients suffering from insomnia, many of them talk of "mind chatter" the condition that manifests continual thoughts which stem from situations in the past or the future. Not one ever talks about thoughts in the Here and Now. The simple fact is such thoughts cannot exist in the Here and Now. It's impossible to live in the past or the future when you are living in the Here and Now. People with sleep problems stemming from stress- related thoughts, are living in the past or future.

If you visit a medical practitioner he or she will prescribe a pharmaceutical product that will blow you away into the depths of Delta sleep. This does not resolve the Mechanical Mind's habit of creating "mind chatter." It's still there waiting for the day you forget to take your pills. Sadly, some elements of the professional world have little regard for thoughts.

As Rosicrucian teacher Joseph J Weed said: "Thoughts are silent and invisible to most and this creates the illusion they are ineffective and not important." The next time you suffer the painful anxieties of thinking and "mind chatter," bring yourself into the Here and Now, and conduct this very effective technique.

Exercise: Dissolving Mind Chatter In Bed

As you rest on your back in bed, eyes closed, mentally watch yourself breathing in and out for a minute or so. Take your time. Never rush an exercise. Then feel or sense your body, the pressure of the bed on your back, legs and feet. Feel your head being cushioned by the pillow. Feel the presence of the darkened room, and again, mentally watch your breathing for another minute. By now you will notice the rhythm of your breathing has slowed.

When you feel calm, decide you are going to observe all your thoughts, and as each thought comes up, decide you are going to put a number on each one. Do not interfere, identify or even think of doing anything with the thought, simply observe it and place a number on it. Let it disappear. Fade away. Then wait for the next thought.

When the next thought comes, observe it and number it, and again watch it disappear and wait for the next thought. You may find the thoughts come fairly rapidly at first and as you observe them, impartially, allow them to fade away.

When you get to about thought number eight, nine or ten, you will discover a very interesting phenomenon starting: the stream of thoughts from your Subconscious is slowing down considerably. Continue by simply observing from your place in the Here and Now.

Keep waiting for the next thought, ready to number it....just keep waiting, enjoying being in the moment....

Somewhere, sometime you will find that you have drifted off to sleep. Practice this exercise for several nights and you will find the hurtful habit of "mind chatter" just slipping away into oblivion. Know that you did not need it in the first place. Beds are for sleeping and healing the mind and body, not for debating stressful issues of the past or the future. Remember stress has no place in the Here and Now.

Incidentally, if your work involves using a computer, and you have one in your bedroom, get it out. You will be glad you did.

THE TYRANNY OF ILLNESS

When you grasp the full impact of Impartial Self Observation and its relationship to the Mechanical Mind, the False Self, and it's connectedness to the past and the future, you are ready to understand pain and illness.

You may have discovered by now that all pain and discomfort is in the past. When you self-remember, when you live in the Here and Now, there is no place for pain and discomfort.

Years ago when I used to join the hordes of downhill skiers at Whistler in British Columbia, I met a workshop student named Alex over coffee one day. "I have arthritis in both legs and my doctor said I would never ski," he told me. "I find something peculiar. Whenever I get on the skis and hurtle down the slopes all the aches in my body disappear. How is that?"

I told him: You are living in the Here and Now, the present moment, the Eternal Now. When you ski, play tennis, climb a rock face, swim in a race – you are doing something that holds your focus on the eternal present, the Here and Now. There is no suffering in the Here and Now, because pain only exists in the past. "It is one of the great secrets – and advantages – of living in the Here and Now," I told him.

"Can you teach me how to do that all the time?" he asked. Over several sessions I did, and the last time I saw him, he was living and self-remembering permanently.

BEWARE OF IDENTIFYING WITH AN ILLNESS

The same applies to any illness, even a catastrophic illness. The greatest mistake anyone can make about an illness is to identify with it. You've probably heard people around you declare: "I'm an arthritic" or "I'm an asthmatic," or "I'm a hypertensive," or "I'm a manic depressive." Mechanically they wear their medical or health conditions like a badge. They wrongly identify with a condition. Start viewing it as not belonging to you. Here's how to do it.

When you are in Here and Now consciousness regard your body as "It." View it as belonging to someone else. This is seeing the body objectively and it brings a feeling of relief, a feeling of freedom.

Never, never identify with the illness. Never say "I am sick. I have....(whatever)." This only adds to your illness. It confirms your illness. Worse, it not only reinforces your negative condition, it actually prolongs it. Relatives and friends – all with mechanical, conditioned minds may accuse you of "denial," because that is their programming.

Essentially, you will accept the illness, but this does not mean you accept it on the level of the False Self, psychologically, emotionally or morally. You accept and observe it impartially in the Here and Now. Watch your illness as a detached observer, knowing that the best way to terminate the illness is to refuse whatever sensation it is manifesting by living in the present, the Here and Now.

You will then see your situation clearly, no longer through a "glass darkly" but objectively. It is when you have dissolved all the baggage and limitations and fears and faces of the Conditioned Mind that true healing can begin. The natural flow of life can start work without opposition or interference.

Every cell in your body remembers itself. It has intelligence. It has a consciousness. It remembers good health, and when you totally accept the condition without reservations, without the mechanical, negative conditioning of the False Self, the body team can start to rebuild and regain the health it remembers.

In the next section of this book, you will learn to unconditionally love your body, and this is one of the most powerful healing techniques you can possess.

HOW TO SEE THINGS CLEARLY

Ralph Waldo Emerson said: "You find men talking everywhere from their memories, instead of from their understanding."

The mind is totally mechanical and it works through energy. It remembers everything you have ever done since before birth. It is conditioned to store all memories on the very simple pleasure-pain system and everything in between. Pleasure memories are stacked with a desire to be repeated, while painful memories are either suppressed in the subconscious or, depending on the aggressiveness of the False Self, kept in an armory ready for combat anytime, anywhere.

Knowledge is one thing. It is a faculty that lives in the mind. Understanding is totally different. When you live in the present, the Here and Now, you don't rely on memories to justify a statement, a feeling. Memories are always there for you as a service, a resource, but they are no longer a mechanical response, they no longer exist as a protection device, an armament of defense, a shelter protecting the False Self.

When you live in the Here and Now, you start to see things clearly. You start to understand why you always reacted mechanically in the past, and you start to see such reactions in a new light. You are no longer asleep.

The ancient teachers claimed that most men and women are asleep. They live in sleep and they die in sleep. Some writers call this a psychic hypnosis. The False Self lives either in the past or the future, which as we have seen, are illusions. It is from these illusions that the False Self dominates with statements that simply are not true – and if they are not true, that means they are lies. Not intentional lies, but untruths nevertheless. Winston Churchill, a master of oratory, who never accused anyone of being a liar, called untruths "inexactitudes" and liars "non-exactitudinarians."

Our daily activities are plagued with inexactitudes that stem from laziness, conceit, vanity, egotism, pride, irritability, cowardice, morality and depravity. "If you don't lie on your resume," say some experts, "you'll fail in getting that job." According to the Society of Human Resource Managers over 53 per cent of all job applicants lie to some extent on their resumes. Three quarters of all college students said they would tell an untruth to get a job.

Even resumes that maintain a strict level of truth, fail to tell hiring officers about who the applicant really is. Resumes are simply lists of accomplishments that the applicant has chalked up over a period of time, but because the system operators are asleep, the lists do not reflect the true character of the applicant.

When you live in the Here and Now and are totally aware, you can read the people around you like a book. When you live in the Now, your intuitive powers are enhanced and you sense the characters and talents of people who come into your environment. Of course, when you do this, do it impartially and work to understand yourself and those people around you.

The day may come when someone writes on a resume "My strength is in self-remembering and living in the here and now."

NOW CONSCIOUSNESS IMPROVES THE MEMORY

Whether we realize it or not, unless there is a physical disability, we all have brilliant, super memories. But it must be emphasized, that you can only access a memory in the present.

Yes, you will hear people claiming "I have a bad memory. I can't remember a thing." The problem is not the memory, it is a case of having poor access. The block is stress one of the faces of the False Self. Stressed people usually have memory accessing problems and the situation, unless addressed, normally doesn't improve. It gets worse. Stress creates dysfunctional memory access.

If you think you have a "bad" memory, consider the following: Do you talk reasonably well? Do you have to think about having a conversation with a friend? Of course not.

When you converse that's your memory working. Your Subconscious mind does it automatically, without you thinking about it. Does certain music bring back nostalgic memories? Can you pick up a glass of water, or write some words without thinking? Ride a bicycle, swim, or walk without thinking? Simply because you can't recall someone's name or you forgot to do something on time, does not mean you have a bad memory. It simply means you were subject to stress or you failed to attach enough importance to those points.

The following is a simple but very powerful exercise that I use with certain clients. It maintains their consciousness in the Here and Now, but it also creates awareness on how events occurred.

Exercise: Backtracking In The Now

First of all, relax comfortably in an easy chair or on your bed. When you are really relaxed, start the exercise. Resist rushing. If you feel compelled to rush, it is highly likely your False Self is urging you. Observe the compulsion. When you are ready, perform the following.

Mentally go back through your entire day. Start by mentally "watching" what you are doing now...relaxing. Then slowly go back, like rolling back a film or video....see or think of yourself lying down...then continue back to coming into your room. Keep on going back through the memories of the day...coming home from work...leaving work....working. Go back through lunch. Pass through the day, examining and recalling all the things you did...but do it backwards.

You will find that as you perform the "thinking backwards" process, it becomes easier, and the details become clearer, and so will your feelings of the memories concerned. For instance, if you recall having an argument with someone, go back through the argument right up to the point when it started. It may be quite enlightening.

Because you are relaxed, you'll notice that the entire event will be much clearer than you would normally recall it, and you'll be aware of the feelings you had. Make a note without judging yourself. Keep on going back through your day, to the point where you woke up in bed.

Once you get used to the process, you will be pleasantly surprised at how detailed the memories of the day are. If you experienced any negative events with other people, you will also see how they ended and more important, how they began. The experience is quite informative. Do this exercise every day for a week, and you'll notice that your memory improves, in fact you will start to feel really good with yourself and your memory.

If you are doing this exercise first thing in the morning, start the process from the point where you went to sleep the night before and go back through yesterday. As with any mind exercise – meditation, self hypnosis, conscious relaxation, take your time.

OBSERVING RELIGION IN A NEW LIGHT

Hakim Sanai, the Sufi poet and philosopher said: *Everyone in the ordinary world is asleep. Their religion – the religion of the familiar world – is emptiness, not religion at all."*

The mainline churches reflect outdated, untruthful creeds, intimidating dogmas and for the most part, boring sermons. Hymns are meaningless in terms of spirituality, and it is little wonder that researchers like the Barna Research Group in California report that people are leaving churches to attend "house churches" for a deeper and more intense experience with God."

The next time you venture into a church, bring yourself into a Here and Now consciousness. Feel yourself seated in the pew. Be conscious of your body, your breathing, and observe, without judgment, how you are perceiving your environment, the people and the clerics.

In this state of being in the Here and Now, focus on how you see, listen and feel to the words and music. Maintain awareness, self remembering throughout the service. Work to understand your perceptions. Do not anticipate the words being spoken by the priest or chanted by the congregation, simply listen in the Here and Now. This exercise will tell you a lot.

TAKING LIFE FOR GRANTED

A successful businessman had built several successful companies and with his wealth had acquired a large, expansive home in the Adirondacks in northern New York State. He enjoyed inviting fellow business people and occasional celebrities to his home. Then, one day, he confided to a friend, "You know, I have been here a year and I'm bored."

"But you have a beautiful home surrounded by some of the most beautiful mountains and luxurious trees," said the friend who was a Sufi. "The air is so fresh. It's exhilarating."

The businessman shook his head. "Whenever I get here, my dreams of this place vanish. My mind is full of the things that happened in the city last week, and what I will be doing next week. There is no peace here."

"There is total peace here," said the Sufi quietly. "You simply don't recognize it."

"Where? Where is it?" asked the man now puzzled.

During the next little while, the Sufi showed the businessman how to relax his mind and body, then how to be totally aware of his consciousness, his inner self. He took him down the road of Impartial Self Observation, and then explained living in the Here and Now. Some hours later, the businessman smiled in amazement.

"There is a wonderful feeling of Being, a wonderful feeling of living in the Here and Now," he said quietly. "I am now at one with this house, and I can feel the stillness, the stillness of the mountains, the trees, the plants, the wildlife. Right now, there's nothing except Being here. How could I ever have been bored enough not to see the beauty of this place...?"

"And yourself," added the Sufi.

"Oh, yes. And myself."

It happens frequently in life. We go to great lengths to build a dream house, and when it's done, boredom, one of the debilitating faces of the False Self overtakes us, and we lose interest and create another dream. We fail to live in the beauty and the ecstasy of the Here and Now.

Exercise: Find Something Beautiful

Find yourself seated in a quiet place where you will not be disturbed, either indoors or outside. Have a flower or a tree a short distance in front of you.

Sense or feel the energy of your inner self. Bring yourself into the state which is simply termed Being. Mentally watch yourself without judgment, opinion, criticism. Feel the spirit of the True Self manifesting in all parts of your body – feet, legs, thighs, abdomen, hips, waist, stomach, chest, hands, arms, neck and head. Allow it to happen. Initially you may feel a warmth occurring, but it will fade into a pleasant feeling of emptiness.

Now, observe the flower or the tree in front of you. Sense or feel the presence of life. The peace. The quiet. Observe what you are feeling. For a few moments, maybe longer, you will feel or realize you are totally in the Here and Now. No future. No past. You realize you are simply Being at one with yourself and the Universe.

When you have finished, close your eyes and work to understand what your experiences were. Do not try to explain them to others.

A note of caution: It may take several attempts to achieve that state of Being. Be patient. Take your time, and you will achieve.

SPIRITUAL AWARENESS

As the False Self dissolves and the True Self comes into its rightful place in your life, and you discover the peace that comes with living in the Here and Now, you will start to find your Cosmic Consciousness manifesting itself. It arrives like the sunrise heralding a new day. Slowly, magnificently you realize that there is a Higher Power, a

Creator, Infinite Intelligence, God, the Source of Your Being, and that it has been there all along. You just failed to see it and that's all right.

Memories of old images, Michelangelo's bearded, fatherly God in the Sistine Chapel, Moses and the Burning Bush, or pictures of a Jesus crucified on the wall of a Sunday School may flicker through. Know that is your False Self attempting to assert itself. Know that the Mechanical Mind cannot exist in the spiritual realms and may block you from making contact.

As you work with your True Self Consciousness, you will receive information that may be completely new to you. Work to understand this new information. Do not attempt to validate the truth of this validation in the old way, the mechanical way, because if you do you will find yourself in a bog of old illusions and frustrations.

Practice the methods learned from this book and you will find that truth is far beyond the mental concepts of the Conditioned Mind. When the information is regarded by the True Self and recognized, you will find an experience beyond measure.

Allow yourself to accept cosmic truths humbly. Protect them as if they are pearls, and if you do feel like sharing them with others, watch your motives impartially as you do so. Always remember that not everyone will be ready to accept new truths, and they may abuse and laugh at you.

Jesus the Gallilean teacher warned his disciples: "Do not throw pearls before swine," which in essence said do not share the teachings with those who don't or can't understand. Ironically, in the end the Teacher shared his mystical knowledge with the wrong people and suffered dire results.

Many people, particularly those with Conditioned and Mechanical Minds consider humility a weakness, but true humility is a wonderful learning experience. The mighty rivers of the world such as the Mississippi, the Rhine, the Volga, the Fraser or the Thames do not flow on elevated positions, but in the comfort of simple, down to earth valleys.

As you live in the here and now, you will find cosmic awareness and psychic energies growing within you. A word of caution: never assume that you know how it will feel, how it will help you climb to higher vibrations. Assuming or imagining such awareness is the old False Self and its conditioned memories creeping back into your life. Allow it to be a surprise and when it happens, work to understand it.

Exercise: The Cosmos And The Tree

Find an open space, a park, a garden—a place where you will not be disturbed. Find a healthy looking tree, preferably one that stands apart from others.

Stand facing the tree, raise your arms and place your hands on the bark. Now, observe your breathing for a minute or so, this will put you into the Here and Now. Feel the presence of the tree. See if you can sense the tree's aura, the tree's energy. It's important not to "remember" or imagine the tree's aura—that's the Mechanical Mind working. Allow yourself to be surprised. When you feel comfortable you are at one with that tree. Take your time. Sense the stillness and presence of the tree. Make yourself a part of the tree, and the tree will share with you the joy of living in the Here and Now. It may also share with you thoughts, feelings and inspiration from the Cosmos.

When you sense you have had enough, thank the tree and withdraw your consciousness into yourself. Take a slow deep breath and as you breathe out speak the words: "Wide Awake!" and be wide awake. Thank the tree for sharing.

All trees, plants and flowers live in the present. They do not dwell on the past or the future. In addition they do not judge, criticize or indulge in opinions as many human beings do. Can you imagine a flower, a beautiful rose looking around and stating: "I am the most beautiful flower in the garden." Strangely, only human beings possess this unique but totally unnecessary neurosis of comparison and judging. By living in the Here and Now, and observing impartially, you are free.

Incidentally, sensations of being in the Here and Now may, at first, only last a few seconds. Persevere and allow yourself to be surprised at your progress.

REFLECTIONS IN CONSCIOUSNESS

As you practice living in the Here and Now you will discover interesting phenomena. Your daily journey through life will no longer be part of the great helter-skelter roller coaster ride, the prison of millions. You become the observer, the watcher of life. Time slows down and takes on a different consciousness. As they say in Zen, you will find you stand on the station platform, watching society coming from nowhere and going to nowhere.

Consciousness is like an enormous mirror in the foyer of a grand hotel. It reflects the passing of life. It sees the coming of famous people and those not so famous. The days come and the days go. The years come and the years go. The mirror reflects but does not identify with what it reflects. That is your consciousness when you live in the Here and Now. You are the watcher, the observer. You are in the world but not of it.

This does not mean to say that you are impervious to the joys and ills in the world. It simple means you can do many of the things you did previously when you were on the eternal roller coaster, but now, you see things differently. The predictable Mechanical World that you saw from the dizzy heights of the roller coaster has changed. Viewed in the Here and Now, your world changes: relationships, the people you work with, your social life, your physical life, and your spiritual life, all take on a different dimension.

Buttons that people used to push to get you to react a certain way, usually negative, no longer work in the Here and Now. You no longer react to events on the nightly news the way you used to, unless you want to. You have a choice on how to react, not because you were expected to react according to the wiles and fancies of society, but because you choose to react. The difference is enormous.

When you live in the Here and Now, you may well see God, your spirituality, death and the afterlife differently. They no longer seem ominous and threatening. You may start to see God in a different light. The monotonous dogmas, the threats of eternal damnation, and the cry of the preacher to "Fear God," are simply reflections in the mirror and you no longer identify with such images seen through a "glass darkly."

When you have let go of many of the faces of the False Self and start to embrace the True Self, when you find your consciousness in the Here and Now, you will discover the ecstasy of what the mystics call the Silence.

BEFORE THE WORD — SILENCE

As you practice living in the Here and Now you may experience an interesting phenomenon. It's called silence. Some people with mechanical minds contort, make strange faces, shudder, even go into mild hysterics when one suggests that a few minutes of meditative silence will change a person's life — their health, their outlook on life, and their spirituality.

Why silence? The Universe was created out of silence. Recall those famous words in the Gospel of St. John: "In the beginning was the word..." Words are sounds — sounds are also light. Go back to Genesis, where God said "Let there be light, and there was light." Each word, each sound can be translated into light.

If you consider music of any description, it all starts with silence. Your speaking ability all comes out of silence. If you didn't have silence, your voice, your speaking, your music would not have shape. It would be difficult to recognize. It's the same with space. If we did not have space around objects we would have great difficulty in discerning them. Space and silence give us power.

Shamans in various parts of the world have known how to create light through vocal harmonics. Internationally known Sound Healer, Jonathan Goldman tells in his books how in a completely dark room in the ancient Mayan center of Palenque, he sounded ancient harmonics learned from Tibetan masters. A soft ethereal light shone sufficiently for the group to see everything. Sound, when it is taken up the scales manifests itself as light.

So before the word, before the light, what was there? The answer is Silence. Infinite Intelligence, the Creator of our Being, has its prime existence in the silence. It is also very much in the word, in the light, but it's also in the silence.

And the ultimate aim of each of us is, as the Yogis say — Union with God or the Creator, the Source of our Being.

Achieving silence is worth seeking. The Path to Silence has many fruits, many benefits and you will discover them along the way.

Exercise: The Candle Of Silence

Make yourself comfortable, sitting in an upright chair, hands unclenched and unclasped on your lap. All the lights in the room are extinguished and in front of you, on a table, burns a simple candle. Allow your eyes to watch the flame. Do not stare, simply observe the flame of the candle. As you watch the candle, mentally observe your body breathing in and breathing out. Sense your body as your feet touch the floor, your buttocks touch the chair.

Sense your whole body in the Here and Now. There is no past, no future, just you, the candle flame and the Eternal Present. If some thoughts manifest themselves, be the watcher, the observer without judgment and the thoughts will dissipate.

Continue watching the candle flame and you will have a glimpse of total freedom which may last that a few seconds, or perhaps a minute or so. This is the ecstasy of what the Hindu mystics call - no-think. If your eyes start to sting, stop the exercise, and practice it another time.

THE LIGHT OF CONSCIOUSNESS

The interesting thing about secrets is that most people, spurred by insatiable curiosity, give anything to know. People love secrets. The interesting aspect is that when you start to share the deep secrets of the Universe with them, they erect a wall and say: "Oh, we don't believe in that sort of thing."

If you have read this book to this point, practiced Impartial Self Observation and felt the benefits and discovered the utter calm and serenity of living in the Here and Now, you will feel the True Self manifesting itself in your life. You'll realize too that Paul's "Glass darkly" is shattered and you can now sit on a bench and quietly watch the majority of people go by each clinging to their illusions on the seemingly eternal roller coaster.

Some people describe the body as the Temple of the Soul, and it's an excellent idea that one should care for the body as a temple, a sacred place. But once the Spirit has departed, it should be allowed to melt back into the physical world.

A lady named Joan sat with me for a spiritual reading. Her husband who had crossed into Spirit some three months earlier, came through and noted she was having a hard time raising money to pay for a monument, a headstone for him. He thanked her for her concern then told her not to worry. "Do something important for yourself with the money," he said. "Think of my old body as an overcoat which is no longer being used. You have buried it at the cemetery, but I am no longer there. I am in a much better place, but I am also with you right now."

It is best to understand that our body is made of material things, which are on a much lower vibration than our Spirit, the True Self. Material things become engulfed in the sea of materialism, but the Spirit lives on.

Like a pendulum, the journey of the Spirit lives on, coming and going, swinging back and forth, being born, living and dying through different lifetimes. Bodies come and bodies go, but the Spirit Consciousness lives on, sometimes imprisoned in that Socratic cave, fearful of the shadows on the wall, sometimes breaking free.

This eternal trek continues lifetime after lifetime until that special light shines. It's called enlightenment. Once this has been achieved, there is no turning back. Once the Spirit is aware of itself, once the delusions, the fantasies, the fears have dissolved and crumpled into the material world, there is no need to come back to the physical. School is closed. Lessons are learned. The student is graduating.

This does not mean that the student cannot return home. The pilgrim can choose to go anywhere, mix and act with old friends and loved ones as if nothing has happened, but the operative word is choose. It is not a mechanical reaction.

There is one more step on this pilgrimage: Learning to love everything – without exception! If you have come this far, you will enjoy the rest.

NOTES TO REMEMBER

o   If one can observe the subconscious mind churning out thoughts – mind chatter – who is doing the watching?
o   While the subconscious mind is a powerhouse of past and present, strangely, it has no concept of the future.
o   The subconscious mind – the Mechanical Mind – finds its fuel in memories. It projects the future based on memories, but cannot tolerate the Here and Now.
o   Time is a necessary illusion. Try measuring it. You can only measure time as the illusion passes through.
o   When you see time clearly and impartially, you will understand that you are being deceived, hurt, and manipulated by the False Self.
o   When you self-remember, when you live in the Here and Now, there is no place for pain and discomfort.
o   As you explore living in the Here and Now, allow yourself to accept cosmic truths humbly. Protect them as if they are pearls.
o   There is only one time – Now.
o   The Yogis ask: "If you're not enjoying yourself right now, when are you going to enjoy yourself?"

3

LOVING YOURSELF UNCONDITIONALLY

"Make love your aim and earnestly desire the Spiritual gifts..."
— Paul the Apostle in 1 Corinthians 14.

"Go beyond reason to love: it is safe. It is the only safety."
— Thaddeus Golas in The Lazy Man's Guide to Enlightenment.

We live in a world where people are desperately looking for answers: Who am I? What am I doing on this chunk of rock? Who is God and why is he allowing people to kill people? Is there a heaven? Is there an afterlife? What's all this about reincarnation?

The hunt for answers becomes more intense. People read books, listen to talk shows, attend endless seminars and workshops, and even go to lengthy retreats given by the gurus who are supposed to know all the answers. They take your cash before they hit you with a complicated formula that they claim the ancients said centuries ago – look within.

People find out lots about metaphysics, psychic happenings, past lives, yoga, Reiki, Zen, astrology, tarot, spiritualism, mediumship, the New Age, Jesus, Buddha, Mohammed and Moses, but they still have their problems. They accumulate vast amounts of knowledge, but unless that knowledge is experienced, unless they feel it deep inside, unless it changes their lives, that knowledge is just that. Knowledge.

The secret to experiencing knowledge is to be in the Here and Now, observing without comment, judgment, opinion. It helps enormously, if you love yourself unconditionally. In the hunt for knowledge, many people fail to find out that its okay to be beautiful, it's okay to love yourself, it's okay to think of yourself as a special being, something unique.

The truth is this. You do not need to ask anyone's permission to love yourself. Just do it. We are reminded of these words by the great teachers in history.

Paul of Tarsus put it very well when he wrote: "Love is patient and kind; love is not jealous or boastful; it is not arrogant of rude. Love does not insist on its own way; it is not irritable or resentful; it does not rejoice at wrong, but rejoices in the right. Love bears all things, believes all things, endures all things. Love never ends." Then Paul advised: "Make love your aim and earnestly desire the spiritual gifts."

Loving yourself is the greatest love of all and we all need to love ourselves – and love ourselves unconditionally. Paul said it almost 2,000 years ago, so where did we go wrong?

It could be that we failed to understand the mechanics of love, the mechanics of positive and negative energies. Perhaps our ancestors attended eternal masses where congregants were, and still are to some extent, exposed to self-guilt and self-rejection by religious organizations that seek to empower the weak. "Let us bring to mind our sins," chants the priest. "He died for my sins," is the hypnotic mantra that ensures the heavy mantle of self-guilt and in doing so, removes any suggestion that one should love oneself. It's little wonder that millions of Christians are unable to follow the core beliefs, the core teachings of Jesus, or his apostle, Paul.

Thus, countless millions told their children: "You don't deserve love," and "You are a sinner." Such chants, repeated freqently were embedded into a child's self-consciousness. Parents saw it as a sign of weakness or a measure of sin to express one's love for a child or an adult.

At an Evening of Clairvoyance a spirit who identified himself as a lady's husband came through. He wore a double-ring of Celtic origin, a point which validated his existence. He gave her several meaningful messages, then said he wanted her to know: "I love you and I always have." The woman jumped up; "We were married for over fifty years and not once did he tell me loved me."

This kind of thing has happened several times in my life as a Spiritualist medium, and demonstrates the lack of love that existed in the old days. It also demonstrates the change that happens when a person passes over into the enlightening world of Spirit. It is indeed a pity that the Love Force, which is no longer hampered in the Spirit World by the chains of the False Self, is so hampered and restricted among cultures on Planet Earth. "Tell and show someone you love them, including yourself," should be a poster hanging in every home worldwide.

People are reported to be leaving the mainline churches in droves, looking, say researchers, for God. They are also looking for love, looking for connectedness. After centuries of spiritual suppression and suggestions of self-guilt, people are finding its okay to love themselves. The ancient teachers were right.

THE MECHANICS OF LOVE ENERGY

The love force is all-powerful, all-Cosmic, all-creative. It exists within us and without. We use and abuse it every day.

Let us ease into the mechanics this way: If your world looks wonderful, you see the world as packed with bundles of positive opportunities, you see everyone you meet as a learning experience, you say "Hello, I love you," to your body as you rise every morning, you are on a fast and high vibration. You can probably teach a class.

But if your world appears gloomy, dark and worrisome, and you live behind a batch of locks on your door, and you secretly curse the day you were born, your vibration rate is pretty slow, and you are in desperate need of some love in your life.

While a lot of people live their lives on a fairly low or moderate vibration, there are many and frequent symptoms that your love energy needs a boost. A common one is that the days, weeks and months are slipping by like an express train. Time is out of control. Simple aches in your body do not get better, they get worse. They spread. You identify with your pain, discomfort and a growing sense of old age, even though your friends tell you that you are still young.

When your vibrations are low, you will receive all sorts of "help" messages both from people around you and also your higher self. You may find yourself rejecting the need for advice, clinging frantically to your world view. View this as resistance. It's one of the faces of the False Self.

Another way of looking at low vibrations is to see life energy as compacted. When a person is living in a compacted energy field, he or she does not communicate much on any level. They may hear others saying that he or she is "closed off."

The opposite of compacted energy is expanded energy. Observe a tulip with a fresh bud. The potential flower is closed. Compacted. There is no indication of what is inside. However, when the bud develops and expands, we then witness a beautiful flower in gorgeous color. When we love everything – ourselves, those around us, those we cannot see, the Universe, the Creator – we come into full expansion.

Observe your resistance impartially and without criticism, and you will find that block fading, your vibrations will start to rise and your flower will start to bloom. Your life, your welfare, is totally in the hands of your vibrations. Events that are happening outside are not your responsibility. What happens internally is your responsibility and you have the power to change it.

LOVE ON THE ROCKS

We live in an age where we like to think that everything is new: technology, psychology, human relationships. We don't like to give credit to history, the past. In spite of the sudden upheaval in family history that has spawned a genealogical industry that creates family trees, we really don't know our ancestors.

What were our grandparents like? We might know from seeming trivia shared by mom and dad that they were hard workers, dressed up and went to church on Sundays, and liked to eat rich food. But what did they read? What did they talk about? What did they think about? What were their plans and ambitions? What made them laugh? What did they like? What were their sicknesses? How did they have sex? Were they romantic? What were their hobbies and pastimes? These people are not strangers on a distant shore, they are your flesh and blood and only a generation or so away, but they might as well be on a distant shore. They are total strangers.

Sit down with your family elders, an aging mother or father, and with a recording device ask them some of the questions we've mentioned above. Ask questions as they come to mind, then transcribe the recording. You'll start to feel your roots.

A lot of people got together many years ago to put you together in this lifetime. Think about it. Accept the fact that you have or had four grandparents, eight great-grandparents, and sixteen great-great grandparents. If you are curious, go back fourteen generations. You will realize that over a million people had to get together to produce you. If you go back far enough, you'll realize that everyone on the planet is related. We are all brothers and sisters.

It's not surprising that millions and millions, probably several billion people on this planet don't love themselves. It's a planetary deficiency, a malevolent disease killing millions of people every year. This is apart from the billions of dollars required to treat people from illnesses that could have been averted or lessened if people had taken the time and effort to love themselves.

The popular media is on the weight-loss wagon promoting various ways for the obese to lose weight through modifying eating habits and exercise. How many of them urge people to love themselves unconditionally? It is almost as if love is taboo.

Many years ago, David Niven appeared in a British movie, "A Matter of Life and Death." They called it "Staircase to Heaven," in America. It was a trial set in Heaven to determine if Niven – a crashed

WWII RAF pilot – should be retained in Heaven, or be allowed to go on living on Planet Earth. Love, of course, brings about the conclusion. I sometimes think how enlightening it would be if there were a Heavenly trial that investigated the origins of why human beings repeatedly ignore the teachings and the urgings of the ancients to love themselves.

As we explained earlier, the Subconscious Mind remembers everything that has happened in your life. It does not miss a thing. It remembers the time when one of your parents or relatives might have said: "If you don't stop crying, we won't love you," or "You are so naughty, how could anyone love a kid like you."

Over the years of growing up, people may have said – jokingly or seriously – "Who on earth would love a creature like you?" or "God doesn't love you, why should we?" There are many more variations, all of which comprise not only mental abuse, but spiritual abuse as well. These pronouncements, because they are either sent or received on an emotional level, take root in the Subconscious Mind, and while you have long ago, consciously forgotten such statements, the Subconscious Mind remembers them vividly. Not only this, it pads the root feelings and gathers any similar or supportive vibrations you may experience along the way. The negative suggestions are intensified.

Mary Y was a client in Vancouver. A 45-year old professional with an old fashioned tightly-cropped brown hair, reminiscent of Victorian religious paintings, she wanted to build up her self confidence. "I'm constantly letting myself down in front of clients and in my relationships – for what they're worth."

"For what they're worth" came over like a wet, heavy blanket so I asked: "Do you love yourself?"

Mary shook her head vigorously. "No! No! Nobody loves me." She laughed nervously. "Even my parents who live next door have never loved me."

I ignored the fact she had not answered my question. "Did your parents ever say that?"

"Oh, no...I don't recall them ever saying that, but I can tell they have never loved me," she said.

In hypnosis we regressed Mary, and asked her Subconcious Mind to take us back in time to an "unhappy" memory. A memory that really hurts.

Mary has just had her fifth birthday. "I'm standing in the dining room and looking into the kitchen," she says. "Mom and Dad are arguing. I'm afraid. It's so hateful! They are yelling at each other."

What are they saying?

"It's all about me. I'm the cause of all their arguments. They don't love me. They hate me and they hate each other." She started to cry in hypnosis.

Are you sure?

"Oh, yes, I'm sure. They don't love me and they regret the day I was born. I know it."

Can you actually hear what they are saying?

"I don't need to. I know."

Mary, you're a little girl. I want you to listen to what they are saying. You can now hear every word clearly. It's happening now. At the count of three, start from the beginning of the argument. One – two – three."

There was silence for almost a minute. Mary's eyes flickered quickly. A frown creased her brow. She started to breath rapidly, then almost as if someone had flicked a switch, relaxed and the frown disappeared to be replaced by a gentle smile.

"Dad doesn't want to go grocery shopping with Mom," she whispered. "They are not arguing about me at all. My God! They are not arguing about me at at all, and I thought....I thought..." She burst into tears and forty years of self-imposed hurt started to flood out.

Over the next few weeks, we helped Mary build up her self-love and positive energy. Each week she would come in and tell of the new relationship she was having with her next-door parents. "They can't understand it," she laughed.

Mary had been a victim of her own Subconscious Mind and a memory that had been suppressed four decades before, but it had been just as strong right up to the point when she had started to really listen in hypnosis and the truth had been revealed.

Many of the suggestions that one picks up in childhood, can be corrected in the Subconscious during adulthood, although many people falsely believe that they cannot change. They come up with feeble, unjustified excuses such as "That is the way I am," or "It's in my genes," or "My parents and even my grandparents thought the same way. It's impossible to change." Such thinking condemns the speaker to an eternal, unncessary hardship.

Self-talk, the powerful chatter that we have with ourselves, has been recognized for many years, centuries in fact, otherwise Paul would not have stressed the case for love twenty centuries ago. Many of the modern researchers and mind-gurus claim 80 per cent of what the average person says is undermining, blocking and self-destructive. When you think about that, it is like carrying a heavy ball and chain around your neck.

There is an old story that tells of two Zen monks traveling to a distant monastery. One was old and wise, the other was a young novice. As they approached a fast-running river, they spotted a village woman standing on the bank. She was confused and upset that she could not get across. Immediately, the old monk picked her up in his arms, waded across the river, and then put her down safely on the other bank. They continued their journey. Much later, as they approached the monastery, the young monk was silent and bothered by his thoughts. "Tell me," he said. "How could a highly esteemed, highly respected master like yourself stoop to carrying a peasant woman across the river?" The old monk smiled. "I put that woman down on the river bank many hours ago. Why are you still carrying her?"

Many people carry the past into their current lives. Someone may regret the death of a loved one and continually ask why. Another person will feel guilty that he or she did not say all the things they wanted to say before a mother or father died. A woman who was savagely beaten by a man and left for dead, eventually recovered, but it was a painful period in her life. The man was sent to jail where he died. Asked how much anger and bitterness she felt against the man, she responded: "That man ruined my life. I will hate him to my dying day." It's heard so many times on local newscasts. A father or mother who have lost a dear one because of the actions of someone else, make the statement: "I will never forgive that person - even to my dying day."

Have you ever noticed how the Conditioned Mind, the Mechanical Mind attempts to justify our behavior? Whenever we feel guilty, bitter, jealous, angry or embarrassed about an event that happened in the past, we carry that burden endlessly.

Be aware: Seek to understand why you retain these burdens from the past. Use Impartial Self Observation and without comment, judgment or opinion, work to understand that burden from the past- and eventually you will be free.

When you start to love yourself unconditionally, you will appreciate that everything that has ever happened to you has contained a lesson-an opportunity to learn. The secret is to recognize it as such. View it using the Impartial Self Observation technique, and you will find that something you considered negative, is in fact a valuable learning opportunity. It is a lesson, a gift for you to learn and move on.

If you feel blocked, inhibited, and sense that it's the way you have been taught to say such things, you should know *you* have the power to change this. Practice Impartial Self Observation. Watch yourself saying or thinking negative self-talk, particularly if such internal talk is prevalent in your life.

Here's an interesting fact: the moment you activate your imagined video camera onto watching this activity, you shine the light of awareness on the problem and it stops. It loses power and slithers away. It dissolves. Observe it without comment.

The Subconscious Mind, your internal biological computer, learns through repetition. If you resist the notion, observe how corporations frequently repeat their advertisements on the media. They know they are changing the way viewers and listeners think. But you can change the way you think by changing your own self-talk, simply by resolving to do it. Talk to yourself positively whenever you have the opportunity, whenever you are alone. Do this powerful exercise.

Exercise: Observe Loving Yourself

When you are alone and feeling comfortable, place yourself in front of a large mirror. Look at yourself slowly and deliberately. Look past your face and deep into your eyes. Feel your own presence. Your own breathing. Your own body. Your own mind. Your own spirit. When you are ready say these words: "I love you."

Now, observe any and all mental and physical responses. How do you feel? What are the reactions? Pain, an ache, an impression of heaviness, panic or a sense of elation? Observe the reactions? Where in your body are they?

If you feel embarrassed, observe the embarrassment and work to understand it. Do not judge it. If you feel discomfort or pain, observe it. Whatever you do, observe it, even if you feel like laughing or turning away. Watch yourself without judgment. If you feel like starting the exercise again, do that, and again observe the reactions. You may need to repeat this exercise over several days. Simply persevere and you will be rewarded.

When you get to feeling totally comfortable with yourself, complete the following. Again, standing in front of the large mirror, feet slightly apart, arms at your side with the palms facing forward. Look into your eyes and in a loud voice say:

"I'M FANTASTIC...I'M MARVELLOUS...I LOVE MYSELF."

Say it aloud three times with determination and vigor. Make it a mantra. Make it a salutation.

This finishes the exercise. Now observe how you feel in body, mind and soul, and observe it all without judgment. You may well feel high on Cosmic energy. Do this every day, first thing every morning, and you will find your days - and your life - are different. Incidentally, a wonderful teacher named Lee Milteer taught me this exercise many moons ago.

MAKING GOOD THINGS HAPPEN

It's a truth: Whatever you imagine in your body, actually happens. If you imagine you're sick, you'll be sick; if you imagine you're well, you'll get well, and if you imagine you are relaxed, you will be relaxed. So, if you imagine you are loved, love will start to play an important role in your life.

When it comes to love, the great teachers knew exactly what they were talking about. Because, when you love yourself, and you love yourself unconditionally, your energy is expanded and good things start to happen in your life. Your flower is blooming.

When you love your body, for instance, your body responds. Listen to someone who is racked with pain and chances are you will hear someone mentally chastizing or vocally criticizing their body.

Whatever you imagine or feel in your body–the body responds. Remember, your body is an extension of your Mind. When you send messages of love and appreciation to your body, it will start to respond. Even if your body is already sick, or in a negative state, send messages of love and appreciation–you'll be glad you did.

Next point, start thinking of yourself as lovable. Start to do lovable things for yourself and others. It costs very little effort to smile at people you meet. The world needs smiles. Give a gift without expecting anything in return. When you are working, think of yourself working for the good of the Universe–and the Universe will repay you.

COMPLIMENT UNIVERSAL INTELLIGENCE

One more thing: If you believe in Universal Consciousness, God, the Creator, the Source of Your Being–and that Source created you, is it not natural that that Source would take an interest in your progress along the path? When you love yourself, and love yourself unconditionally, that is a compliment to the Source of your Being.

When you fail to love yourself, because people said you should not because you are unworthy, or because someone once did bad things to you, that is a bit of an insult to the Creator, but as the Creator does not have an ego problem, do not let it worry you. Resolve to start loving yourself.

Remember, first and foremost, you do not have to ask anyone's permission to love yourself. Just do it!

Exercise: Releasing The Burden

Whoever told you you were not lovable or worthy may have created a burden for you. Recall the story of the two Zen priests? To release others, relax yourself in meditation and go into your Special Place in your mind. When you are settled, ask your Subconscious Mind to remind you of who told you that you were not lovable. The voices will come up quickly. Identify the main ones. Next, have the people concerned stand in front of you in your Special Place. Then quietly inform them with these words:

"I don't condone or approve of what you said to me, but I do forgive you."

Say it three times, then add:

"My psychic connection with you is broken. Go your way and go with love and light."

End the meditation by sitting in the silence for a few minutes.

All through the meditation, it is important that you maintain an Impartial Self Observation mode. Note how you feel, particularly afterwards. Work to understand yourself.

(Note: If you do not know how to perform basic meditation, there are how-to instructions in the Appendix at the back of this book.)

WALKING ON THE LOVING PATH

Changing the world is a very admirable objective but it carries the power to drive you crazy. It's also one of the faces of the False Self known as possession. So, be careful as you walk the loving path. If you want to change the world, or your view of the world, start by changing yourself which is the object of this book. As you change, people will notice and perhaps follow.

Incidentally, don't share these thoughts of loving yourself unconditionally with others–particularly negative thinkers, because they'll pull you down. Jesus, the greatest of all teachers, told us not to throw pearls (of wisdom) before swine. You get the idea?

Today, there are many great teachers out there carrying the words of the ancients. So where does one begin? Start by deciding that you are worthy. When you are alone and quiet, stand in front of a mirror, and gaze into your own eyes, and say out loud: "I am lovable...I am lovable...I am lovable. I love myself." If you find it difficult at first, that's natural. Impartially observe the fact you find it difficult. You may well find there's a whole lot of negative thinking to overcome. Persist with the impartial observation, and you will be rewarded. You'll find your intuitive gifts guiding you to the right teachers.

In my work as a hypnoanalyst I often ask people: "Do you love yourself?" The responses are as varied as the weather. If you ask yourself this question and you feel hesitant, uncomfortable, turn on your video camera — and conduct Impartial Self Observation. Work to understand yourself in every way.

The benefits of loving yourself are impressive, and if you do not love yourself, you are missing one of the most beautiful powers of the Cosmos.

These words may sound strange, but they are true. Whatever you do in your life, at work, at home, at play, always love yourself, and you will find good things starting to manifest in and around you.

Remember this important point: You don't have to get anyone's permission to love yourself. Just do it and enjoy. Another point: You do not need to tell people that you love yourself. The ones who are close to your vibration will instinctively know that you are living on a love vibration. Their higher selves, their psychic faculties will observe a blooming, an expansion of your energy.

EVERYTHING IS A LEARNING EXPERIENCE

As you tread the path to finding the True Self, be hungry for learning. Practive living in the Here and Now and observe everything and everyone that comes into your environment. Be a watcher. A learner.

From the time you rise in the morning, watch everyone. A loved one with whom you share breakfast. Casually watch them as they move around, listen to their oral and silent communication. Do it impartially, without judgment, criticism, comment. Watch the gas station attendant, the bus driver, the people on the train, the people walking past you on the street, your colleagues at work, your friends in the evening. Simply watch and listen. Observe. There is not one person you meet during the day that does not have a lesson for you to learn

As you do this, you will realize sooner or later, you are living on a different level, a different vibration. You are developing an esoteric awareness. Initially you will wonder where a whole bunch of strange thoughts are coming from. Be the watcher. Observe them without attachment. Know that you are picking up thoughts and feelings of others. Observe your reaction to this. If this causes worry or a feeling of guilt, impartially observe these faces of the False Self that linger on.

As you progress and your own flower starts to bloom and you realize your energy is expanding, allow yourself to know you are living in the Here and Now, and that it is natural to love yourself unconditionally.

AN EGOTIST IS LIKE A BLACK HOLE

Some people might tell you that loving yourself is egotistical. That's conditioned thinking. People are trained subconsciously to make such statements. In fact, like in many things pertaining to the Conditioned Mind, the truth is exactly the opposite.

An egotist is similar to a black hole in space. An egotist will take your love and attention, absorb it and give nothing in return. When you love yourself, you become a source of love, and you radiate that warmth outwards and share it with others. It is like a beautiful light within you. The interesting thing is that you do not have to tell anyone you love yourself, people will sense the fact. Their higher awareness, their intuitive powers will relay your change of con-sciousness. Sooner or later, close friends will tell you quietly, "You've changed. I don't know how, but you've changed."

Some people still living with the Conditioned Mind may tell you that it is not right to love yourself. "You are a sinner," they may chant mechanically.

First, you should know that the Creator made you, and if you decide not to love something that God created, that is akin to being an insult to the Creator, but as the Creator does not have an ego, do not worry about it. Just go right ahead, ignore the Mechanical Minds and love yourself anyway.

While you're at it, send the egotists unconditional love — they need it. Do it mentally and quietly. Just don't tell them because they'll suck you in like vampires. Do these things and you will be glad you did, because you'll be making great strides on the spiritual path to embracing the True Self.

THE POWER OF WATER

Ever since the dawn of time, humans have been fascinated with the power of water. One of the outstanding qualities about Planet Earth – is the abundance of water. It's a unique feature that makes our blue planet stand out among other members of the solar system. Just over seventy per cent of Earth is covered by water. The remainder is terra firma. Coincidentally, seventy per cent – give or take a few points for your age and makeup - is about the water content of human beings.

We were taught in school that liquid water is H2O, the most abundant molecule on Earth and that it is transparent, odorless, tasteless and impossible to describe unless it is in an environment – a lake, waterfall, fountain, river and a sea. In a nutshell it is the simplest compound of the two most reactive elements in the Cosmos – two hydrogen atoms attached to a single oxygen atom. It might appear simple, but like many simple things, it contains incredible powers.

Water has always held a special place in our society and our lives. A lack of it causes drought, parched earth, crops fail, and people suffer shortages. Water also possesses enormous destructive powers. Witness torrential rains and floods that devastate lands, villages and towns, and tsunamis or tidal waves that roar across oceans destroying property and thousands of lives.

Water has another side. It's used for cleansing, cooking food, irrigating crops, helping plants and trees grow, and it also helps to irrigate our bodies.

The human body creates havoc when it is dehydrated. Early or mild dehydration may include dry, warm skin; dizziness; or cramping in the arms and legs. As dehydration increases, signs may include: a flushed, red face, urine production dwindles and it may be difficult to pass. The eyes become sunken and black, irritability is pronounced, and if symptoms are not addressed, dehydration can trigger shock which can affect blood flow in the body and brain, and cause death. And all because a lack of water. Health experts tell us that without an average of eight glasses of water each day, our bodies start to dry out and malfunction.

Water has other qualities too. I like to think of these qualities as mystical. Walk beside the ocean, a lake or a beautiful river, perhaps in a meditative mode or living in the Here and Now, you will feel the energy – it is calming and pacifying. It seems to have an aura of peace and tranquility...and when one experiences that, you simply feel good. You will feel at one with the world and the Universe. When I first started studying and practicing metaphysics in Vancouver, I used to participate in a walking meditation along English Bay. I found the water energized my mind, body and spirit to conduct lectures. Today, I walk and take in the energies of the St. Lawrence River separating the United States and Canada.

THE HEALING POWERS OF WATER

Ancient civilizations knew the value of water. Many had healing wells and healing baths – places where people came to be healed. Today, there are healing wells and water sources in many parts of the world. For instance in the little Mexican town of Tlacote the well receives about 10,000 visitors a day, all bent on carying away a can or two of the now-famous miracle water. There is another healing water source at Nordenau, east of Dusseldorf, in Germany. It was discovered in the cave of a disused slate mine in 1992. Today the town is packed with people in search of healing. And of course, there is the legendary Lourdes, a town in the high Pyrenees in France.

Yearly from March to October the Sanctuary of Lourdes is the place of mass pilgrimages from Europe and other parts of the world. The spring water from the grotto is believed by some to possess healing properties. An estimated 200 million people have visited the shrine since 1860 and the Roman Catholic Church has officially recognized almost 70 miracle healings. Such is the power of water.

The healing power of water: Is it faith or is it a fact? Can water heal?

When I first started the study of metaphysics, my yogi teacher told me about Prana, the life force of the Universe. It is Spirit, the motivating force of life in general; the life force sustaining the body. The breath is an external manifestation of the subtle life force.

He told me how to change the power of water by accentuating or increasing the prana within it. Anyone can do it, and I share it with you now.

Exercise – Charging Water

Take a glass of water either from the tap or bottled water. In both cases, prana is at a low ebb. You may sip it to test the flatness. Now, take another glass which is empty, and hold up the full glass above the empty glass. Now, pour the water from one glass into another so that it passed through ten or twelve inches of air. Do this five or six times. Now, sip the water and notice any changes. The pranic levels will have increased, and if you drink the water during the day you may well feel an increase in energy.

Is this faith or fact? Did we change the power of water by intentionally increasing Prana? This raises the intriguing question – can our thoughts and actions change the constituency of water? The answer? Absolutely!

PRAYER CREATES BEAUTIFUL CRYSTALS

Japanese scientist Dr. Masaru Emoto back in the 1990s first started investigating water. He developed a technique using a very powerful microscope in a very cold room along with high-speed photography, to photograph newly formed crystals of frozen water samples. He discovered that pure spring water created beautiful crystals, while chlorinated tap water or polluted water from rivers were malformed or failed to form crystals at all. And like snowflakes, no two crystals appear the same. Each one is different. Dr. Emoto tested the waters of Lourdes and found a stunningly beautiful asymetrical crystal coming from the healing waters.

In his experiments Dr. Emoto discovered that crystals of poor water, were substantially changed for the better if they were exposed to beautiful music. There was more to come. The Japanese scientist found that if you prayed over the water, or wrote pleasant, loving words on the water container, the crystallization process changed. In a nutshell and as incredible as it may seem: Water responds to positive thoughts, voices and positive sounds. In effect water molecules possess a consciousness.

And it doesn't matter what language is used – Japanese, Korean or English, the results were very similar which means it is the thought that carries the message.

Dr. Emoto believes that all these changes are based on Chi or Qi which is the oriental way of the Prana talked about in Yoga – the life force. He believes that the life force changes according to the consciousness of the observer. The fascinating findings of Dr. Emoto, including hundreds of photos of water crystals, are contained in his book "Messages from Water."

People all over the world are now experimenting with water. My partner, Betty Lou, had a sore thigh muscle. We filled a container, placed a note with the words "Healing and Love" underneath it and left it overnight. The next morning, she rubbed the water onto the sore muscle and a few hours later – her leg was free of aches and back to normal.

Some journalists, notably one from the New York Times, ridiculed the idea of talking to water, but a scientist has shown – that if you talk to water – or even pray to water – it changes positively.

Exercise: Love Water and Reap Benefits

The Subconscious Mind learns through repetition. Practice this and allow it to become a positive habit – you'll be glad you did.

Whenever you are about to have a drink of water take time out and for a few moments observe the water lovingly. Know that you are in the Here and Now, and either mentally or aloud make the following declaration: "I love you. I appreciate you. I am at one with you."

Make it a ritual. Keep water handy in your environment. By your bed. On the breakfast table. In your car or in your pocket or purse as you ride the bus or train, on your desk or place of work – everywhere, keep water, and love it unconditionally. If you feel some resistance, impartially observe the resistance and learn from it. Do not judge yourself.

Know that as you drink the empowered water, each of the molecules flows into your body and is absorbed by the system, which as we mentioned earlier is around seventy per cent water. The new molecules carry the love message. They spread it. They share it. The whole system is infected with the message of love. What a wonderful phenomenon.

Go get yourself a glass of water.

In addition, do this when exercising your green thumb. Talk lovingly to the pot of water you intend to pour onto house plants. Better still, put a note on or under the pot that says: "We love you". In the morning irrigate your plants. In a few days you will see the difference. If your love message through water can impact plants, think of what it can do for your body.

If you hesitate and perhaps feel you're on a fool's errand, recognize the hesitations as blocks from the Mechanical Mind and perform Impartial Self Observation. Simply watch such blocks without judgment, opinion, etc.

MEDITATION — THE GATEWAY TO SILENCE

Meditation is an altered state of consciousness. It is a beautifully relaxed state that will help a person to relax, let go of stress, allow dreaming and imagery and perhaps have a great understanding of their own spirituality. But unless you work from a base of silence, it will all be based on memory, the mechanical mind – the False Self.

Many people ask: "On what should I meditate?" Meditation has no subject. If, when you meditate, you can observe yourself meditating, you have not allowed your True Self to manifest true meditation — which is silence.

We live in a world where society teaches that our days must be full in order to achieve a sense of completion. Unfortunately, this takes its toll on human beings mentally and physically. Such living is stressful, so called "nervous breakdowns are common," and antidepressants are the daily diet. Mental health is one of the major problems besetting our health institutions. When you live in the Here and Now and are fully aware of Being, you cannot be depressed or suffer a so-called "nervous breakdown."

The teachings of the ancients which are reflected in this book, impartial self observation, watching oneself, learning from oneself, dissolving the totally unncessary False Self, the negative ego, should be on the curriculum of every school, college and university. Loving yourself unconditionally should also be taught everywhere. But alas, all these things are neglected, even considered taboo. The mainline churches in their insecurity blocked these and other teachings that could benefit mankind's spiritual progress, and chose to control and suppress.

While in meditation watch to see if there are any fears or feeling of insecurity that come up regarding silence. Keep on observing yourself when you meditate and eventually you will enter the silence. If you expect to find God, Infinite Intelligence, the Creator there, that's the False Ego recalling memories which are illusions.

Observe your expectations, and go back and work on this book again. When you no longer expect mechanical gods, conditioned idols, programmed angels, you'll be at one with everything in the silence.

The best meditation practice is to expect nothing. The moment you expect something, you are inadvertently judging, using past experiences, past memories, past limitations to create something. Allow yourself to be in the Here and Now, floating in the abyss, the space of nothing. Allow whatever wants to come, to come. If you slip into a memory, gently observe it without judgment, and allow it to fade away and continue to simply be.

LOVING YOURSELF IS SIMPLE

Love yourself and see everything as a learning experience. As you love yourself you will start to see the world and your place in it in a different light. The world has not changed, and neither has your place in it. The change has come about through the way you see and react to it. The Conditioned Mind, the Mechanical Mind is losing its power over you. You are free.

If you feel you have a problem with any part of loving yourself unconditionally, focus on the problem. Ask yourself: "Why am I feeling this way? Allow the answers to come up without comment, opinion or judgment. As you watch the process you will probably find the answer is somewhere in the realm of Self #1– the False Self. Even as you use Impartial Self Observation, the problem – the face of the Ego Self – will start to diminish.

How does one start to love oneself? It is relatively easy. Just do it. Say: "I Love Myself." If you notice yourself hesitating with those three words, observe your hesitation, work to understand it, and you'll find any hurdles along the path disappearing.

When you use Impartial Self Observation on any emotion, any hesitation, any feeling that wants to say "You can't love yourself," observe the emotion observe the block, always without judgment, criticism or comment. It will pave the way for you to get out of the Cave, get away from the Mechanical Mind, excape from the False Self which is holding you prisoner.

You will discover the futility of self-judgment, and as you feel a presence of self-fullfilment, you will discover there is no need to judge people close to you, loved ones and those in important relationships in your life. As you progress with living as your True Self, living in the Here and Now, you will find it is all right to love yourself unconditionally and your life evolves.

No expectations. Simply let it happen.

FEELING THE PRESENCE OF THE COSMOS

As you feel your love for yourself and your environment growing, it is likely you will become aware of the Cosmos, Infinite Intelligence, the force that makes energy move.

You may recognize the force as God, the Creator, the Source of Your Being. Your Mechanical Mind, the False Self may well bring up images of the fearful God of the Old Testament, or the "Father" God referred to by Jesus, the God of Love.

Work to understand the Cosmos, the Source, the motivating force that makes a tiny seed grow into a towering oak tree, or produce a beautiful, dazzling flower. Work to understand that our Universe is a mass of energy fields in which all the molecules and atoms vibrate in the own way, in their own fashion.

Never be afraid to ask questions. If you realize a fear in asking questions, observe the fear and allow it to dissipate. As you observe anything, love yourself for everything you do and you will always do the right thing.

As you live in the Here and Now, impartially recognize the world around you, your environment, the sunlight on the flowers, the grass and the trees, as you observe the birds fluttering from branch to branch, rearing their young and singing their hearts out, you will start to expand your consciousness.

You will observe the night sky and the planets, the stars, the galaxies, and wonder what is out there and wonder where God or the Creator is. Someone will tell you that God is hidden, and maybe they will suggest the Latin word "occultare" which means "to hide." You may wonder where God is hidden?

If God is hidden, you are hidden too. It's somewhat frustrating to know this, but one does get used to it: You cannot see yourself in the Here and Now, only the past. For instance, if you look into a mirror, you are seeing yourself in reverse. Even as you look, the image is a reflection of you that was a moment ago. This is why many people express a dislike for photographs of themselves. They are not used to seeing themselves directly, only in reverse through a mirror.

If you resort to having a regular video camera showing you "live" on a television screen, there are so many milliseconds delay in seeing yourself. It is impossible to see yourself in the Here and Now. We are all hidden from ourselves. As you realize this, impartially observe your reactions and learn.

While we are discussing something we cannot see, or understand, think about the Cosmos, the Universe. In spite of scientists and astronomers coming up with detailed calculations, no one has any idea of how big or how small the Universe is. As a mystic once said: "We may be like a walnut sitting in the hand of God."

You may have been told by a well-meaning Sunday School teacher that God created the world in six or seven days, and some scientist later told you about the Big Bang Theory.

The Big Bang Theory is the dominant scientific theory about the origin of the universe. According to the big bang, the universe was created sometime between 10 billion and 20 billion years ago from a cosmic explosion that hurled matter in all directions. The theorists claim that everything is expanding, which is grand stuff. The problem is they have not figured out from where the Universe is expanding, and more importantly, to where it is expanding. And more important than that, what was in the space before the Universe was created.

The Hindu thinkers who have been around longer than western scientists, believe that there is no such thing as form, that everything is infinite. It is only in the human mind that we look for security in knowing a beginning and an end. As Huston Smith pointed out: "The West likes form, boundaries that distinguish and demarcate. The trouble is that boundaries also imprison – they restrict and confine."

Observe these boundaries, they are much like Socrates Cave, and see them for what they are, and they will gradually disappear and leave you free.

ALLOW YOUR TRUE SELF TO ENJOY THE MOMENT

Supposing you woke up one morning and you could not remember anything. For a start you would wonder who you were. Next you would wonder where you are. As you climb out of bed, you see through the window a big yellow orb coming up over the horizon. You are amazed. You cannot say the sunrise – for that is what it is – is beautiful. The phenomena creates an interesting feeling inside your chest, inside your stomach. You wonder what the feelings are, because you cannot remember having them before.

As you live right in the Here and Now, as you read this book right now, all of your interactions, all of your feelings, all of your thoughts are based on memories. Memories give you a foundation, a base on which you can make comparisons, judgments, analyze things. A functional memory is important, but when that function becomes obsessive, it can restrict the joys of your life in the Here and Now, and the joys of living as the True Self.

Exercise: Living In The Moment

Find a quiet place where you can sit and see the world around you, perhaps a seat in the garden or a park. Be conscious of your body, how it is seated, how it is feelng, how it is interacting with the seat and how your feet feel with the ground. Be aware of the presence of your clothes. Notice your hands, unclench them if they are clenched. Be conscious of your body breathing. Don't try to change anything, simply observe without judgment or comment.

Now focus on a living object around you. A flower, a bush, a tree. Sense the presence of the tree. Do not look for happiness or unhappiness because these will trigger mechanical memory functions. Simply allow yourself to be in the presence of that item of nature. Observe how you feel. Make sure you are not comparing it with anything. Accept what you see and feel as purely and totally new in your life. Observe your own feelings without comment. If old comparisons pop up, observe them as the watcher, and they will recede. Always work to enjoy the moment as your True Self. When you feel ready, take a slow deep breath and as you breath out simply say "Wide awake."

Now, you can perform this Living Now exercise anywhere. You may do it while walking through a forest, hiking a mountain trail, walking by the sea or a lake. You can also do this when you meet someone for the first time, or you attend a play or a concert. You may hear people around you commenting: "That wasn't as good as the play they put on last year." Understand that they are victims of their own memory. Allow yourself to be thrilled by the phenomenon of the moment. Observe your feelings.

Practice these things and you will find your life changing. The more you observe, the more you become the watcher, without criticism, comment, judgment, the more you will find yourself living in the Here and Now.

Socrates' cave, the roller coaster, Paul's Glass Darkly which plagued and hampered your life in the past will be gone. As you walk the path to higher learning, the more you will find you can Love yourself and the Cosmos unconditionally, and you will be at one with the True Self.

GENERAL THOUGHTS

- o   Understand that you do not have to ask anyone's permission to love yourself. Just do it.
- o   Never identify with aches, chronic discomforts or a sense of growing old. Observe them from the True Self in the Here and Now.
- o   If you think change is impossible, you are condemning yourself to the past. Impartially observe all resistance to change and see the difference.
- o   Whatever you imagine in your body actually happens. Learn to love yourself unconditionally and reap the benefits.
- o   The True Self is free of mental sickness.
- o   When you love yourself unconditionally including every cell in your body, your body responds.

o Love water. Your body is 70 per cent water.

o When you love yourself, you become a source of love, and you radiate it outwards and share it with others.

o Love the fools who taught you not to love yourself.

o Forgive the fools who taught you to "fear" God. The operative word is "Love."

4

PATHWAYS TO COSMIC CONSCIOUSNESS

Walt Whitman described it as "ineffable light, light rare, untellable, light beyond all signs, descriptions and languages." He was referring to a state called Cosmic Consciousness, a term used as a classic book title and subject by Canadian psychologist Dr. Richard Maurice Bucke.

Bucke reviewed the works and teachings of some of the world's greatest writers, orators, artists and religious thinkers and what is known about their lives, and came to a fascinating conclusion. They were all enlightened to various lengths and levels. Some of those discussed in detail include Gautama, Jesus, Paulus, Plotinus, Mohammed, Dante, Saint John of the Cross, Francis Bacon, Jacob Boehme, William Blake, Walt Whitman, Lao Tse, Socrates, Benedict Spinoza, Swedenborg, Emerson, Thoreau and Ramakrishna Paramahansa.

Dr. Bucke explained that the phenomena comes suddenly and without warning, usually when a person is in the early thirties.

Sometimes it is a sensation of being immersed in a flame or rose-colored cloud, and there is a feeling of ecstasy, moral and spiritual illumination in which, like a flash, there is a clear conception of the Universe. You feel as if you are part of a breathing, living Universe and that there is no death and life is eternal. You understand the principle of life and unconditional love, and you see clearly through the futility of the human ego. It comes in a flash to many or it may come as a gradual dawning over time. Paul of Tarsus was blinded by Cosmic Consciousness on his way to Damascus.

Mystic Jacob Boehme put it this way: "The gate was opened to me ... in one quarter of an hour I saw and knew more than if I had been many years together at a University ... I saw it as in a great deep in the internal; for I had a thorough view of the Universe, as a complex moving fullness wherein all things are couched and wrapped up." There is no deciding factor as to which is best, a speedy illumination or allowing a slow immersion.

PATIENCE IS THE KEY IN ALL THINGS

There is no fixed way to Cosmic Consciousness, but various sources have indicated different paths. In this one the student, the pilgrim on the path has three tasks, three levels to attain before waiting for the rose colored cloud, the mists of ecstasy, the blinding light of Cosmic Consciousness to envelop the True Self. In addition to no fixed way, there is also no fixed feeling, and no fixed time. Patience is the key. If you feel impatient at times, impartially observe the impatience and you will find a lurking face of the False Self. Watch and it will fade into obscurity.

THE THREE LEVELS TO THE TRUE SELF

The three levels are given to you in this book.

Level One: Self-Remembering.

Being conscious of the True Self. Clearing Paul's famous "Glass Darkly" – the False Self. Dissolving the Negative Ego from your life. Understanding that all those many faces were illusions gathered along the Highway of Life.

Level Two: Living in the Present.

Understanding that the past and what happened yesterday and years ago are only memories – memories that fueled the False Self, which in itself was an illusion. Understanding that the future too, does not exist, and that too, is only an illusion. Still, in order to maintain direction in a material life you need to learn from past illusions and plan for the future. The important aspect of Level Two is practicing and learning to live in the Here and Now. Know there is no other time than Now.

Level Three: Unconditional Love.

Loving every cell in your body – and I mean every cell. Know that it is all right to love yourself unconditionally, and you do not have to ask anyone if it's OK – yes, even God. When you love yourself unconditionally, you have love for humanity and the cosmos. It cannot be otherwise.

At this stage you will understand what the mystics and the mystery schools have been teaching down the ages that human beings and the Cosmos are one. True unconditional love is a natural phenomenon, the basic force of the Universe.

THE TRUE SELF IN EVERY DAY LIFE

You may well be thinking at this stage: "How can I live my life like this? How can I work, have a relationship, maintain my friends and colleagues?"

Have no fear. You will find that as you work through the power of your True Self, your "I am," you will be able to live on whatever level, whatever vibration level your material or social life requires. It is always your choice. You are no longer in Socrates' cave or riding the eternal roller coaster. Nobody else can tell you what level of consciousness to live your life. You are free to create and enjoy your life the way you desire.

Understand that you will find you simply fit in because you understand – you understand yourself and you understand others. A word of caution. Never attempt to change others by what you have learned and experienced, unless they specifically ask for information. And then only give them what they have asked for. This is an ironclad rule among mystics and metaphysicians. Remember we spoke of Jesus and his famous quote: "Do not throw pearls before swine."

If you love yourself unconditionally, you will not think of boastfully talking of your progress in spiritual development. If boastfulness ever arises, observe it impartially and the desire will dissolve.

WELCOME TO ALPHA

Cicero, the Roman orator once said: "A happy life begins with tranquility of mind." You may have noticed in many of the exercises in this book that you have attained an altered state of consciousness. It is probably what we call the Alpha state.

The brain energy, like all power, works in cycles. If you are in a high-stressed, deadline- pressured work, your brain cycles will be quite high, somewhere around 25 to 30 cps – that is cycles a second. If you are a meditator and are generally relaxed you'll be down around 10 cps. Here's a chart to give you a picture.

Brainwaves generally come in four categories: Beta, Alpha, Theta and Delta.

Beta 13 - 40 cps occurs when you are under pressure, either mentally or physically and neurons fire abundantly in the brain. The Beta state includes exercising, working to achieve peak performance, playing competitive sports, taking an exam, giving a major presentation. In Beta you are in high mental alertness and a high level of concentration. Negatively, you may have a feeling that there is not enough time in the day. Beta is the dominant state during the day for most adults. However, Beta should not become an obsession, because like most things in high gear or overdrive, stress sets in accompanied by eventual disruption of the mind and body. Learn to take breaks.

Alpha 8 - 13 cps. When in Alpha, one is relaxed, in a light meditative state, day dreaming, or experiencing that Sunday morning "I don't have to get up" feeling. This is an excellent state for practicing mind-changing creative imagery or auto-suggestion and positive self-talk techniques. It is beneficial for developing intuition. Most psychics, spiritualist mediums, medical intuitives work in this state. It is also a good state for automatic writing and studying. This is a right-brain working mode for artists, writers and creative people. Alpha was discovered by Austrian psychiatrist Hans Berger in 1908.

Theta 4 - 7 cps. This is the basic stage for sleeping. It's referred to as the twilight state and brings such phenomena as dreamlike imagery, inspiring thoughts, and raises long forgotten memories. Regression-ists use this state when exploring suppressed or hidden memories. It's also the state for deep relaxation or deep meditation where one is not asleep. The mind can be aware but the body feels heavy, if there is any feeling at all. Remote viewing, astral projection, and rebuilding body energies are all available in the Theta state. In this state you may feel your mind expanding beyond the boundaries of your body.

Delta 1/2 - 4 cps. Delta is deep sleep state and is excellent for healing. Hypnotists use this state for people in pain or as a mind anesthetic. The brain slips down into Delta several times during the course of the night, refreshes and rebuilds, and then returns to Theta. Certain levels within Delta trigger the release of Human Growth Hormone, beneficial for healing and regeneration.

LIVING IN THE ALPHA

When you walk the paths to higher awareness, the True Self, the Cosmic Self, and persevere you will find yourself living and working for longer and longer periods in the relaxed Alpha state. There will be times when you break out for work or exercise, but generally you will find you can do most things in Alpha.

One benefit becomes obvious. You do not use up valuable ener-gies so much in Alpha as you do in Beta. Beta is an energy zapper.

Harold was a senior manager in a forest products company on the west coast. His job required that he make presentations at service club and chambers of commerce luncheons. "I'm terrified," he said. "I know the ins and outs of this industry, but I get so stressed in front of large groups. I think I'm going to blow a valve. I get stressed two or three days before I'm scheduled to talk."

He came from a quiet spoken family where his father said at almost ever meal: "Little boys should be seen and not heard." In therapy we reframed the root memory, worked to understand and forgive the father, then we trained Harold to live in the Alpha state.

"It's amazing," he told me. "I stay in light Alpha – totally relaxed – until I get up to speak. Then I allow myself to slip into Beta by taking a deep breath, and saying 'Good afternoon. It's wonderful to be with you.' It's great. People come up afterwards and praise my oration skills."

When you live in Alpha and come up to complete a task in Beta, then return to Alpha, you will find your mind and your body working like the proverbial Swiss watch.

Incidentally, most children up to the age of seven or eight live in the Alpha state, and as they learn the False Self from their environment, they move from Alpha into Beta full time. Sometimes the transition is not smooth. Some children are subconsciously drawn back to Alpha, perhaps suffering Alpha-withdrawal, and develop such conditions as ADD – attention deficit disorders.

You might consider teaching your child some of the techniques given in this book, particularly in Sections one to three. They will, sooner or later, discover their own silence.

THE SOUND OF SILENCE

In all of this you will ultimately find a silence. Through these techniques and exercises it may have already come into your life. As you practice meditating in the Here and Now you will start to find that silence. Acknowledge and welcome it gently. It is quiet, a peace, that pervades everything, whether easily recognizable or not. As you find it, you may feel suspended, unattached or incredibly light. Observe your feelings.

Pure sound comes out of silence. Without the base of silence, the foundation of music and words would be lost and have no meaning.

Imagine a radio that is bringing you the news but the message is distorted by dozens of other sounds. The news is difficult to understand because it is not coming out of silence. Imagine now the news coming out of silence. You are comfortable because you hear every word and understand each one. It is the same with music or any other communication based on sound. Sound without silence is sick and distorted.

It is a fascinating phenomenon that all matter in the Universe has a molecular structure – that's you, me and everything – right through to infinity. And each molecule has a sound. If you analyze or listen to those molecules and atoms, you will discover that each one has energy, each one has a sound. And all light has a sound structure that comes out of the silence. Thus every atom, every molecule, every cell in our body has a sound, perhaps not the traditional sounds of music that we recognize, but each one has a sound.

Internationally known, Colorado-based sound healer Jonathan Goldman says the human body is a *"celestial orchestra filled with sound."* The pulse of the heart, respiration, circulatory system, the nervous system, brainwaves, all create sounds within the human body – sounds, which for the most part go unnoticed by our consciousness.

SOUNDS WITHIN YOUR BODY

Dr. John Beaulieu discovered body sounds while sitting in an anechoic chamber at New York University. An anechoic chamber is a completely soundproof room resembling a sensory deprivation chamber. After reading about the experiences of the American avant-garde composer-philosopher John Cage he decided to experiment.

Cage found that he had heard two sounds while in the chamber, one was a high-pitched sound and the other a low-pitched sound. The engineer he was working with informed him that the high sound was his nervous system, and the low sound was his blood circulation.

Excited by this discovery John Beaulieu then sat in an anechoic chamber for five hundred hours over a period of two years listening to the sounds of his own body. He began to correlate different states of consciousness with different sounds of his nervous system. Being a trained musician he noticed that the high-pitched sounds of his nervous system consisted of several sounds in different intervals. Then one day he brought two tuning forks and tapped them. Immediately, he observed that the sound of his nervous system realigned to the sound of the tuning forks. From this Dr. Beaulieu developed Biosonic Repatterning.

These body sounds are subtle, but the nervous system sounds can be heard when you are under stress. Depending upon your stress level, the sounds can become a ringing in your ears. For most people, body sounds can only be heard if you listen quietly.

Dr. Beaulieu advises one to find a quiet place, sit or lie down, close your eyes and focus your awareness on the sounds inside your head. Listen for the high sound. When you listen closely you will discover that sound consists of two distinct pitches. These pitches originate from your left and right brain hemispheres. These pitches change in frequency, volume, and pitch depending on your state of consciousness.

THE SOUNDS OF CREATION

This raises the question, and many believe that this is so, that God, the Creator, Infinite Intelligence, created the Universe out of the silence with sound. Is this what John refers to in the Bible when he says: *"In the beginning was the Word, and the Word was with God, and the Word was God"*?

The ancient writers wrote for an ancient audience and "word" was more suitable than sound. But in truth, the biblical quote should have been: *"In the beginning was the Sound, and the Sound was with God, and the Sound was God."* God created the Universe and everything in it from the sound which came out of the silence. If God was in the silence, then that has to be God's base, God's domain – silence!

Does Paul refer to this cosmic silence when he writes in Philippians: *"And the peace of God, which passeth all understanding, shall keep your hearts and minds through Christ Jesus."* The peace of God is silence.

LEARNING FROM A COSMIC MASTER

Jesus, as I have mentioned before, was a great teacher who taught the mystical teachings of the ages, which are reflected in the Bible. That these teachings such as the Sermon on the Mount go over the heads of many people is a sad commentary on the fact that the mainline Christian churches, which profess to promote these teachings, have failed miserably in their mission.

Jesus, as Dr. Bucke says, was embraced by Cosmic Consciousness. We know he was a medium, a clairvoyant and an incredible teacher.

For almost two thousand years, staunch Christians have talked about the second coming of Jesus. Supposing, just supposing, the NBC news desk in New York received a call from a Pennsylvania resident who proclaimed: "Jesus is here and he's talking to crowds of people in the meadow. It's the same stuff he said in the Bible."

The news editor would yawn and politely say "We'll follow it up," promptly forget it and turn to the yo-yo activities of Wall Street. But supposing he had sent a TV crew to interview the man called Jesus, and broadcast it, public reaction would instinctively be disbelieving. Scientists would declare: "Bring him in for testing and analysis." Skeptics would declare: "It's a trick. He's a con." And the theologians would say, he doesn't match the Jesus we know. All in all, the Second Coming of Jesus might turn out to be a fizz.

Sad to say, most people today would not recognize Jesus, the Christ. Why? Simply because the orthodox image has become so distorted through an unfortunate process of idolization developed over almost two thousand years. A similar idolization has developed over the Bible, claimed by many fundamentalists to be the absolute or infallible word of God. One wonders why so many men have actually changed the word of God.

UNDERSTANDING PAST SHADOWS

Many people who are now spiritually motivated to be independent and study higher learnings on their own, may find they are still plagued by shadows of the orthodox teachings instilled in them when they were young.

As one progresses along the path to the True Self it is difficult to ignore such intimidating, fear-inspiring concepts as The Last Judgment, the horrors of Purgatory, Hell and Damnation, Vicarious Atonement and the promise of Salvation if Biblical tenets are maintained. If, as you travel the path you find these shadows bothering your progress, observe them impartially. Watch them and work to understand them, and they will no longer bother you.

Remember, Jesus did not teach such concepts, they were all developed by Christian leaders in the Fourth and Fifth centuries who molded the early church and practiced effective methods of crowd control. Jesus taught the principle of Universal Love.

Bluntly, Jesus was a very difficult teacher to follow. The disciples – actually, Jesus called them friends – and most of the 120 in the Upper Room were endowed with the Holy Spirit or Cosmic Consciousness. After Jesus had made his transition into the Spirit World, they could heal and perform similar "miracles". But after several generations, Christian leaders, aware of a return to Paganism, and unable to perform miracles and teach as Jesus had done, branded everyone "sinners," and adopted such fearsome concepts that can only be termed gross spiritual intimidation.

THE MYSTICAL TEACHINGS OF JESUS

Jesus was the wayshower, the teacher, the mystic. He taught the wisdom of the ages, much of it contained in the Sermon on the Mount. In fact, the entire mystical teachings of the ages regarding the Conduct of Life are contained in remarkable style in the Sermon on the Mount.

Take the parable of the sower and the seed. The lesson of sowing and reaping is based on the Law of Cause and Effect. Understanding the law is critical for all of us, because we are not punished **for** our negative deeds (some call them sins), but **by** our deeds. We create our own happiness or unhappiness. You would be surprised how many people readily blame others for their unhappiness. All the great teachers have recognized and taught this.

Living in the present, the Here and Now is a must from the sermon where the teacher looks at anxiety, and asks *"Can any of you by worrying add a single moment to your life-span?"* This is the essence of the first part of this book: observe your anxiety. The teacher also advised: *"Stop Judging, that you may not be judged. For as you judge, so will you be judged."*

Another teaching: *Do not worry about tomorrow; tomorrow will take care of itself."* This part advocates the need to stop being anxious and live in the Here and Now, which is the subject of the second part of this book.

Another classical teaching by Jesus, which, incidentally is to be found in many of the world's major religions: *"Do unto others what you would have them do unto you."* It is known as the Golden Rule.

Prayer is a supplication to God, the Creator, the Cosmos. Here we have him teaching creative imagery. "Therefore I tell you, whatever you ask in prayer, believe you have received it and it will be yours." Creative imagery is not a discovery of the current century. Jesus taught it in Palestine almost two millennia ago.

There was more: Make a prayer and expect an answer. *"Ask and it will be given to you; seek and you will find; knock and the door will be opened to you."* If you have limitations, ingrown fears about following these instructions, go back to the beginning of this book and start reading again.

It's a miracle that the essence and truths of these profound Cosmic teachings withstood the long editorial debates, numerous rewrites, and tortuous translations imposed upon the Bible, of which today there are over 2,000 versions.

Jesus was a healer, clairvoyant and medium and the New Testament is full of such occurrences, which many in wonder, and ignorance, might describe as "miracles," or "supernatural" events.

Students and practitioners of metaphysics and spiritualism know and understand how and why such events are manifested through the natural laws of the Universe. Andrew Jackson Davis, the Poughkeepsie Seer wrote: *"Nothing, therefore, can occur in the vast empire of the universal creation opposed to, or transcending the principles of nature."* Paul Solomon the Virginia Beach philosopher, said it another way: *"Everything in God's Universe works according to God's Universal Laws, including God, Jesus and yes, you and me."*

The term "miracle," is a misnomer. It is simply an event or occurrence that is currently beyond our understanding and comprehension. We need to work to understand the natural laws and the important Gifts of the Spirit. Recall the words of the Teacher: *"Greater things than these shall ye do. Go then and do likewise."*

Another Biblical person endowed with Cosmic Consciousness was Paul of Tarsus who said clearly: *"Make love your aim and earnestly desire the spiritual gifts,"* and he named them: wisdom, knowledge, faith, healing, prophecy, distinguishing between spirits, and speaking in tongues. He added: *"It is the same God who inspires them all in everyone."* One wonders how long the mainline churches are going to wait before they start teaching these spiritual gifts.

This has been the advice of the teachers since time immemorial: love yourself. Jesus said it too, in fact the God of Jesus is a God of Love, unlike the angry, jealous, hurtful God of the Old Testament. When Christian fundamentalists and others claim to be Christian and follow the teachings of Jesus, it fails to be evident.

THE POWER OF NATURAL LAWS

Working and living and loving within the natural laws is critically important for living with the True Self. Imagine driving up a one-way street the wrong way. The consequences could be severe. Imagine attempting to swim across a fast flowing river. You may tire and expire before reaching the other bank. The answer? Go with the flow and gradually work your way across.

A great Spiritualist instructor and author, Marilyn Awtry recently wrote an excellent book on the wonders of Natural and Universal Laws. It's called "The River of Life: How to Live in the Flow."

The Bible is not a credit to the mainline churches. It is a credit to the early writers of Jewish history, and the early Christians before Emperor Constantine. In spite of countless rewritings, the Bible is a history of man's struggle for greater awareness, better understanding and a fuller, richer way of life. It is a chronicle of man's spiritual evolution. For those on a spiritual path, the Bible is a magnificent resource for spiritual, higher awareness and psychic development. Chances are, your church will not tell you.

The Bible carries with it a particular phenomenon - it is multi-dimensional. It is written for different levels of development. If you are a fundamentalist or orthodox Christian, you will only see what you want to see. If you are a developing psychic or medium, you will see other things. A student of deep mysticism and Cosmic Consciousness will read other information perhaps not seen by the others. The Bible has many levels of information and teachings.

Emanuel Swedenborg (1688-1772) the Swedish visionary said the scriptures must be understood in a spiritual or mystical sense. According to Bucke, he was illuminated with Cosmic Consciousness. Swedenborg was a highly respected scientist and engineer until about age fifty-five when he began to see visions, develop clairvoyant faculties and claim the power of communicating with spirits – "discarnate souls." He talked of talking with God and various angels, and asserted that his interpretation of the scriptures in a book *"The Word Explained"* was dictated to him in automatic writing by Spirit.

Swedenborg wrote extensively of his spiritual and theological experiences, and in the mid-1750s it is easy to recognize that his thoughts and freedom in writing were severely influenced by the different Inquisitions that had raged in Europe for several centuries. One wonders what he would have written without those influences.

THE ILLUMINATION FACTOR

But to return to the silence – the peace – the peace that passes all understanding. Gandhi noted: *"It is possible to live in peace."* Many people have innocently gone to war to fight for peace, but the peace of which we speak, and the peace to which Gandhi refers is the peace that resides within your consciousness. It is the peace that is found on the path to superconsciousness. Some call it "Illumination," and others "Cosmic Consciousness."

Writers through the ages have talked about this phenomena and it has been referred to by people involved in most forms of religious belief. Many people believe Cosmic Consciousness comes about through devotion to some form of Deity, or by chanting some creed or mantra that Illumination will come upon them. Others believe that meditating on a daily basis will bring about Cosmic Consciousness. It becomes quite depressing that after such devotions one leaves the church, temple, synagogue or spiritual development class to find that one is still on the seemingly eternal roller coaster and the clouds of stress of the world are still as menacing as ever.

Some fall into the "holy" trap. This is when the crafty False Self, the negative ego actually manifests from its vast arrays of memories, supposed faces of Cosmic wisdom in order to protect its existence. The False Self is incredibly crafty and will perform all manner of distracting strategies to protect itself.

Lao Tsu in Hua Hu Ching wrote: *"Not all spiritual paths lead to harmonious Oneness. Indeed, most are detours and distractions."* This emphasizes the need for the dissolution of the False Self. Until it is immobilized and ineffective, Paul's "Glass Darkly" will obscure any clear vision.

Illumination or Cosmic Consciousness is a phenomena above worship, creeds, or ideas or impressions of God, the Creator. If a picture of God flashes into your mind – chances are it will be based on memory – and that's your False Self still working. Observe the memory impartially and it will dissolve.

Cosmic Consciousness is not as rare as Dr. Bucke or subsequent writers have supposed. Many philosophers, writers and poets have embraced Illumination and so have priests and men and women of all walks of life. Some fail to realize what has happened, they simply feel out of line with people in their enviroment, and withdraw into silence. Others, such as Swedenborg, wrote to pacify the spiritualists of the time and the mainline churches.

MEETING JOSEPH, A SPECIAL PERSON

Some years ago, I visited a facility for mentally handicapped people in western Canada to see a staff member. While there, I noticed an elderly man sitting quietly in a chair apparently gazing into infinity. His aura was beautiful.

"That's Joseph," said the staff member. "His family had him committed. They think he's insane. Totally unbalanced. His brother thinks he's an alien."

"What do you think?" I asked.

"Me?" he said surprised. "Joseph is a genius. He understands life and he understands the Universe. He is totally in touch with nature and he talks of the oneness of all. He loves everyone unconditionally, even the family who put him here. He says that when he sleeps, he visits other civilizations in the galaxy, and he also talks to angels - spirits."

"Spirits?"

The man nodded. "Joseph has distinguished visitors. Einstein, Ben Franklin, Conan Doyle, Abraham Lincoln, Bucke, Mackenzie King, Mesmer - they have all been here to chat with him."

"How do you know?" I asked, smiling.

"My dad came through, and Joseph relayed a lot of messages. Then he said: Your father tells me to tell you - don't forget 1415," said the man. "Then I knew it was Dad. He was always talking about 1415, Henry the Fifth and the Battle of Agincourt."

I wanted to know why Joseph was in this facility. "He's just fine," said the man. "Once I offered to get him out and take him home, but

131

he told me he was just fine here. He said: There is peace here – peace beyond all understanding."

Some people might say that Joseph had a problem. One might say he was unable to quietly hold Illumination or Cosmic Consciousness to himself, and go out and perform as his family environment expected him to perform. But Joseph had found his place of silence, his monastery, and was having a ball.

Spiritual development, while it has its benefits and blessings, also has its costs. I conduct regular spiritual development classes – meditation, higher awareness and spirit communications – and I warn new students. "If you have differences already between yourself and your partner in life, spiritual development may well expand those differences. The best solution is to get your partner to attend and learn and in this way, you maintain a more equitable balance in vibrations.

A PROBLEM WITH DR. BUCKE

I wonder if you noticed the section we wrote on Dr. Bucke and the people he mentions in his book "Cosmic Consciousness." There is a problem which can be summed up in two words: no women. At least, no women are mentioned as possible people attaining Cosmic Consciousness until the last section of the book. Then there are only three in the "Lesser, Imperfect and Doubtful Instances" category.

Bucke was a Canadian who, for many years, was Medical Superintendent of the Asylum for the Insane, in London, Ontario. When he wrote his classic book he was still in the Victorian era which, like the Bible and some religions labeled women as second class. The good news is that there have always been women who were embraced by Cosmic Consciousness but because of religion, tribal and societal thinking and conditions, never openly acknowledged the fact.

Men could, with relative ease, display their Cosmic awareness through their writing, either in books or in poetry, or in their work as missionaries and counselors. With women, their Cosmic awareness drove them to seek safety in convents or remain silent.

If Dr. Bucke were alive today and writing a new edition of Cosmic Consciousness, he would probably include such women as: the 19th century American poet Emily Dickinson; Antoinette Bourignon, the 17th century Flemish mystic; the 14th century Catherine of Sienna who saw love as the supreme reality of the Cosmos; and Teresa de Jesus (Avila) the 16th century Carmelite nun who wrote an ecstatic story of the soul in *"The Interior Castle."*

Then there was Hildegarde of Bingen, the 12th century German mystic who wrote: *"These visions which I saw, I beheld neither in sleep, nor in a dream, not in madness, nor with the eyes of the body, not with physical ears, nor in hidden places, but wakeful, alert, with the eyes of the spirit and with inward ears, I perceived them in open view and according to the will of God."* In addition there was Battistina Vernazza, an Italian monastery prioress in the 16th century who wrote meditations, poems and songs on the means of attaining illumination.

Some illuminaries were imprisoned at times for their beliefs and statements. Such was the case of Madame Guyon, otherwise Jeanne Marie Bouvier de la Mothe. In 1676 she felt the call of the Cosmos and entered a life of religious devotion to God in which she taught complete indifference to such things as eternal salvation. Her mystical experience focused entirely on God and was accepted as normal.

Kathleen Raine, a much publicly honored British mystical poet whose poem *"Exile"* showed a vision of eternal love through all created things. She was a poet who believed in the sacred nature of all life, all true art and wisdom. William Blake, another on Bucke's Cosmic list, was her teacher in his writings, and she shared his belief that *"one power alone makes a poet - imagination, the divine vision"*. She crossed into spirit in 2003, aged 95.

Katharine Trevelyan in her *"Fool in Love"* which she called "An *Autobiography of a Natural Mystic"* described how she saw God and *"Light streamed down from the sky such as I have never beheld."* For the British-born daughter of a Government minister, illumination occurred after hitch-hiking alone across Canada in the early 1930s, living for an unhealthy spell in Nazi Germany, and then having a "nervous breakdown" in England when her marriage ended in divorce.

BREAKING FREE FROM A MIXED WORLD

Women who were embraced with Cosmic Consciousness in those other centuries lived with two major problems: religion that suppressed any inclination to mysticism and illumination, and a male-dominated society that scarcely tolerated anything individually spiritual.

Today, we live in a society that is breaking free from the bonds and shackles of the past. More and more people are realizing that they can be in charge of their own spirituality.

I am of the belief that we were all born with Cosmic Consciousness. Some might call it Enlightenment, Higher Consciousness, Buddha Mind or Christ Consciousness. It is a state that is inborn in us and it never goes away. It becomes blocked and imprisoned by the False Self and is only able to see through the Glass Darkly.

As we mentioned earlier, children when very young, live in the Alpha state, but they also manifest higher consciousness or Cosmic Consciousness at various times and in various ways. These include things they say, the quiet times alone, or in the telling of dreams. Parents who suspect a child of True Self consciousness, are advised to keep a journal, a diary of activities and comments made by a child. Such parents may not have much time, because by the time the child is six, seven or eight, that special consciousness becomes lost. It is over-shadowed, overwhelmed by adulthood and the barrages of habits, conditions, limitations, and practices which influence the young ego and create the False Self. Paul's Glass Darkly manifests itself, and Cosmic Consciousness, the True Self takes a back seat.

THE LIGHT IS ALWAYS THERE

It is an awareness that sets someone free. They ask the question: "Is there something better? Is there a light?" The answer, plain and simple: The light is always there.

Jesus the Galilean, and other teachers over the ages have described the way to the True Self and Cosmic Consciousness as passing through a "narrow gate." It is challenging.

As recently as August 2007, Pope Benedict speaking at Castel Gandolfo said: *"The way to eternal life is open to all, but it is 'narrow' because it is demanding. It requires commitment, self-denial and mortification of one's own egoism."*

Take note: "mortification of one's own egoism." That is the very subject of this book. Death, elimination, the dissolving or crucifying of the False Self. It is indeed a pity that the Holy Father cannot see clear the way to teaching practical techniques to the masses.

A READINESS FOR ILLUMINATION

Self Remembering, dissolving the False Self, Living in the Here and Now, and Loving Yourself unconditionally, will bring about a readiness for Illumination. As I said before, it may happen in a flash, or it may manifest itself over a period of time. Have patience. Do not imagine what it will be like - that allows your False Self to throw up a few old memories. Your False Self has no idea, no concept of spiritual or cosmic enlightenment.

The illuminated man or woman sees and feels that all the world is alive. It's a living organism that is pulsating with life and intelligence. They see, hear and feel the joys and the sorrows of the world around them. Humanity is part of all animal life, it is also part of the Earth, the forests, the mountains, the deserts, the lakes, the rivers and the seas. There is no part from which the illuminated person is detached. They feel identity with all of life and they understand it.

Like Joseph, the illuminated person has no bitterness or anger for his brother, even though the brother's actions could have been hurtful. The illuminated person always seeks to understand and

135

knowing this, he feels the drive, the inclination to all the attributes of higher life. The illuminated person lives in the Here and Now, and has no fear because fear is a face of the False Self which becomes sterile history as the illuminated person moves on.

The illuminated person will not impose his thoughts and feelings upon others struggling on the roller coaster, attempting to leave Socrate's cave, or struggling to clean Paul's Glass Darkly. He or she will, if the struggler genuinely seeks help, and genuinely displays a need to move towards the light, will answer any questions and provide assistance. But the illuminated person is not a missionary, an evangelical imposing a religious order. Cosmic Consciousness takes a person safely beyond the shackles of religious dogma.

The illuminated person will, if asked, teach the inquirer how to understand himself or herself, how to shed the guilt, the anger, the bitterness, the jealousy and all the other countless faces of the False Self. The inquirer will be helped to find – or better still, observe the True Self, that higher power, that spirit that dwells within. The illuminated person has no fear of death because he or she knows there is no such thing, only a transition of spirit consciousness.

EXPLORING HIGHER CONSCIOUSNESS

In this exercise you will be able to focus on the Here and Now, and experience a consciousness separate from your body. First of all, place your body in a relaxed, reclining position. Close your eyes and mentally watch yourself breathing in and out. Don't try to change anything, simply watch your body breathing.

Now, be totally conscious of your body. Observe how your body is feeling, how it is reclining, how your arms are resting at your sides. Observe your fingers and thumbs, and if clenched, relax them. Observe how your legs are resting, your feet. Now mentally observe your head and shoulders.

When you are totally comfortable tell yourself: *"I am in the Here and Now, and I am my True Self."* Say it several times until you are completely comfortable with it.

If an extraneous thought pops up, observe it impartially until it fades away.

Again, tell yourself: *"I am my True Self and I am completely independent of the body. I am not my body, but the True Self, a spirit."*

As you say this several times, think of your body as a shell, useful and comfortable, but simply an instrument of the True Self, the real You.

Think of yourself as an independent being, using the body to accomplish your time on Earth, and you have full control over it.

Now, allow yourself to focus on the True Self. You may mentally chant slowly the words *"I am, I am, I am,"* or if you wish, slowly chant the Universal Buddhist mantra *"Aum."* This is the sacred word that means God, the Highest. Chant either one a number of times, listening to the sound in your body. Make the "Aum" long and drawn out, like a music hum. Start with your lips closed, then as you chant sound mmm-ahah-ohohoh-oo-mmmm. The tone should last ten to twenty seconds. Pause, and then start again. You may well feel the energy building in your body.

As you meditate you may well experience the sensation of being out of your body, and of returning to it when its time to conclude the exercise.

One of my early teachers was Yogi Ramacharaka who lived in India in the late 19th century. His teachings were brought to America by a student, Yogi Baba and written for publication by an American William Walker Atkinson at the turn of the 20th century. While I was studying the dozen or so books, a slim, brown entity Yogi Ramacharaka, white hair flowing, came several times to my classes and was seen by various students. The above exercise is based on his teachings.

BELIEF IN SPIRITS AND THE AFTERLIFE

There comes a time in spiritual development when you see and hear things that conflict with your old belief systems. I say old because your limitations may still be existing even as your consciousness expands.

You may still ask yourself: How can I believe in spirits and the afterlife?

Consider this. If as a believer in the Spirit World and the Afterlife, you go through your life confident in the knowledge that there will be something better when your term expires on Earth, you will enjoy a comfortable life with comforting expectations.

If however, you declare "I don't believe that sort of thing. That's rubbish!" you'll go through your life living with that limitation, perhaps wondering if there is such a thing as the Afterlife. And when you get to the Afterlife – the Spirit World – you'll say: "I could have had the comfort of believing in the Afterlife all through those years on Earth."

If, however, you don't believe in the Afterlife, and you've taken some delight in shooting down believers in your lifetime, and there is nothing after death – just nothing! – you'll never have the satisfaction in knowing that you were right.

And if you are a Spiritualist and a believer in the Afterlife, and after death there is nothing – just nothing – you'll never know that you were wrong. But all through your life you will have enjoyed the comfort of believing in the Afterlife. Believing in the Afterlife is a bet you cannot lose.

Whatever you feel about spirits and the afterlife, observe the feelings, and if you hear voices from your past, authoritative voices like family or teachers, listen to them and work to understand why they said such things.

EXPERIMENT TO MAKE PROGRESS

Illumination and Consciousness of the True Self, otherwise known as Cosmic Consciousness, is a state of Being that enables one to stand firmly and be strong in mind and spirit. As goes the mind and spirit, there goes the body.

You will find all your senses, your power centers, otherwise known as the chakras, will perform as you have never experienced before. You may well pick up people's thoughts and feelings. You will know when the phone is going to ring and who it is. You may see shapes and forms of loved ones in spirit coming and going. You may also have an encounter with an ascended being from the realms of spirit. Do not be surprised, simply accept the phenomena, work to understand it, and move on. As you walk the pathways of life you will hear truth emanating from all the different colors of life. Your vision and understanding will be clear, particularly your vision of spirit.

You will feel the desire to experiment, to travel in your mind, to learn of higher values from sages still on Earth and also in the Spirit World, the astral states. You may also feel a great desire to write and share your knowledge with others on Earth.

EACH DAY IS A DIFFERENT CREATION

As you begin each day, living in the Here and Now, enjoying the freedom and release from the old False Self, the negative ego, you will find yourself in tune with the Universe, God's Cosmos, and you will feel the pulse of that super energy. You may feel alone, but never lonely. Fear is gone from your life. Your thoughts will pose questions that fly off like darts into space.

The Cosmic traveler does not plan his or her day. Yes, there will be commitments, mostly mundane things like work, shopping, making appointments with the dentist or the auto service station, and joining a friend or colleague for lunch. A Cosmic day brings a myriad of events that produces learning, understanding and wisdom. There is not a person you encounter who does not have a contribution to make to your learning. Your presence will also contribute to their learning and understanding. It may well not be on a physical level but a higher consciousness level, a metaphysical level.

You are awareness. The Cosmic Self, the True Self is awareness. There is no "I am aware." You cannot practice the old method of "I am" and hope to be aware. The "I" that cannot make you aware is volitional, it's a thought from the old Mechanical Mind, a memory, and it is quite helpless in creating a genuine awareness.

True awareness that comes after the powers of the False Self have dissipated is multi-dimensional. It has no sides, no form, no limitations, no shackles, no fears, no pain or suffering, no Glass Darkly. As Cicero, the Roman orator said at the beginning of this book: The Spirit is the True Self.

IMAGES OF GOD, THE ABSOLUTE

As you tread the path to the True Self and open the doors for Cosmic Consciousness, it is best to forget all the conventional images your mind has ever picked up on God. In fact, if you can imagine God, the Creator, the Source of your Being, the Absolute, understand that that is what someone has told you and there isn't a snowball's chance in hell that it is true. Even people who claim to be endowed with Cosmic Consciousness, have extreme difficulty in describing their feelings when close to the Absolute, or Infinite Intelligence as the Spiritualists call it.

And yet, many people feel that there is an overall presence of God, the Absolute manifesting itself in the world and the Universe.

A mystic will look from a window, see and feel the presence of God in the trees, the babbling brook, the deer grazing in the far off meadow, the birds in the hedgerows, the dewdrops on the daisies, and the puffy white clouds drifting lazily across a perfectly blue sky. A country lane. If that satisfies your hunger for God, that's fine.

But if you wish to experience more, you will have to delete your limitations about God, the Absolute, in things that you might consider un-godly. A concrete sidewalk, a highway, a towering skyscraper, a hamburger, a high speed train, a computer, a book – if God made the Universe, the Cosmos, and is in everything that you consider beautiful, then God must be in everything. There can be no exceptions. If you feel that God has limitations, observe your feelings about God. Work to understand them and broaden your horizons.

Students ask: "How do you see God, the Creator in everything? How can He be in everything?"

First, forget the He, and the Father. Think back, if you were a preacher, a teacher of religion two thousand years ago, and your audience comprised simple fishermen, you would not attempt to discuss Cosmic energy, Natural Laws of the Universe, the Life Force in everything. Ideally, you would have a meaningful symbol for the Creator, the Absolute. Hence, Jesus used the Father. Nice touch.

SEEING GOD, THE ABSOLUTE ON A BEACH

One story that effectively demonstrates the presence of one God everywhere was told by Yogi Ramacharaka in his "Advanced Course in Yogi Philosophy and Oriental Occultism." I have shared it with students many times.

You may do this in reality or the imagination. Find a sandy beach that stretches for miles to the horizon. The tide has recently gone out leaving much moisture on the sand. You kneel down and realize there are many tiny bubbles sparkling in the sunlight on the beach – countless millions, perhaps beyond number.

You peer closely at one bubble. You can see the reflection of the sun shining in that one bubble. The spirit of the sun is in the bubble. The sun is giving its light, its warmth, its energy, its substance, its cosmic energy to the bubble, it is there and yet it is not there.

As the Yogi says: "So that while the sun is in the drop, it is in the heavens – and while it is in the heavens it is in the drop." He calls it the "Divine Paradox," which explains the many which is one and the one which is many – each being real, each being apparently separated and yet really not separated. Meanwhile the sun shares its energy with countless millions of drops or bubbles on the beach, and yet there is still only one sun, and it still remains in the heavens.

The spirit of the sun is in the bubble, but there is an unbreakable link with God, the Absolute. Work to understand this, and you'll start to grasp and appreciate Cosmic Consciousness.

IN THE BEGINNING...

As you find your way off the roller coaster and start walking the path to discover your True Self and Illumination and perhaps your Cosmic Self, you may find yourself asking questions about all of this. Know that all of the texts and exercises in this book are options, possibilities, a maze of openings upon which you can venture. There is no fixed path. Various teachers will claim their ways are best. Some will even really zap you with "These teachings come from the Highest."

You may declare to them and to me: "I don't believe a word of all this. It's nonsense."

Great! Forget everything! You're on the path!

Love, Light and Blessings.

A NEW APPENDIX

MEDITATION TECHNIQUES
FOR RELAXING AND LETTING GO

When you relax on a regular basis, perhaps twenty minutes every day, you'll find some beneficial aspects occurring in your body. Conscious relaxation allows the body to relax and physical stress diminishes. Your breathing becomes easier. The body needs less oxygen. The heart muscle relaxes and your pulse rate is reduced. The heart has longer to rest in between pumping blood. In some cases, conscious relaxation will reduce blood pressure. Conscious relaxation allows an acceleration of natural healing, and there is an overall feeling of well-being.

According to the experts, on the mental level the average person processes well over 100,000 thoughts a day. In round figures, that's about two thoughts every second of every waking day. When one is stressed, mind chatter, as it is called, accelerates. When you relax on a regular basis, mind chatter is reduced. This is, perhaps, the outstanding advantage of adopting a regular habit of self-hypnosis or conscious relaxation.

As stress levels diminish, concentration becomes easier and more effective; your learning capacity expands, and you find your ability to create and achieve goals is enhanced. Conscious relaxation

143

allows your intuitive powers to work better, and there's a better feeling of time, a better feeling of Self. The following techniques are simple but very effective.

You will learn or come to the conclusion that whatever you imagine in your body actually happens. All you have to do here is imagine you are relaxed and let it happen.

SYSTEMATIC RELAXTION

Find yourself a quiet place where you will not be disturbed. Close your eyes and focus on your breathing for a minute or so. This alone will start the relaxation process. Do not try to change anything. Just observe. Next, address different parts of your body, thus: "My feet are relaxed and comfortable....My feet are relaxed and comfortable." Say the instructions slowly, as if you have all the time in the world and imagine that your feet are becoming relaxed and comfortable. Never rush meditation, self-hypnosis or simple relaxation.

Next: My ankles are relaxed and comfortable...My ankles are relaxed and comfortable." Simply take your time and slowly work up through the different parts of your body right up to the top of your head.

When you reach the top of your head say: "My whole body is relaxed and comfortable....My whole body is relaxed and comfortable."

This exercise works extremely well but it also demands focusing. You may well feel your body becoming heavy or even not there. That's normal. Enjoy!

One other point: You may during the process drift off to sleep or "trip-out" as it is called. When you return to your conscious mind, continue your systematic relaxation.

When you feel relaxed throughout your body, go to the section marked *Sanctuary of the Mind, A Special Place.*

MUSCLE TENSING

If you are not afflicted with muscular disorders, you may want to know about the relaxation technique called "Muscle Tensing." This is particularly useful if you sense your body is resistant to relaxation. Do not do this if you are prone to arthritis, rheumatism or fibromyalgia.

Lie down in a place where you will not be disturbed, legs side by side, arms at your sides. Start with your feet. Tense all the muscles in your feet, imagine them getting tighter and tighter. Hold it for at least five to ten seconds, then mentally tell yourself: "Let go!" and feel all the muscles relax.

Next do the same for your calf muscles, then your thighs. Next move to your abdomen, your stomach, chest, arms, hands, then neck and shoulders. Conclude with tensing all the muscles in your face. You may end the process by tensing all the muscles of your body – hold them tensed for five to ten seconds, then tell yourself: "Let go! Let go!" And let go of the tension. You'll feel much more relaxed than when you started.

When you are relaxed and comfortable, go to the section marked *Sanctuary of the Mind, A Special Place.*

COLOR RELAXATION

Find yourself a quiet place, either sitting up or lying down. Close your eyes and focus on your breathing. Mentally watch yourself as you breathe in and out. Do not try to change anything, simply mentally watch the process for about a minute.

Now, imagine or think you are seeing colors. If you have difficulty imagining or thinking of colors, see them as flowers or plants, flags, a paint box, or as colored walls. I heard of one person who had seven swimming pools, each one a different color, and they imagined themselves swimming through each colored pool.

Focus on the colors listed below. Hold each one for 10 to 20 seconds, then change it to the next color. Do it in this order.

Red – Orange – Yellow – Green – Blue – Purple – Violet

When you have reached violet you will notice that your body and mind are relaxed comfortably. Once again, it is critically important that you do not rush this exercise. Take your time. Enjoy the colors. Make them rich.

When you are relaxed and comfortable, go to the section marked *Sanctuary of the Mind, A Special Place.*

PORE BREATHING

This is another useful technique for relaxing. It may sound unusual at first, but it can be very effective. It is based on a Yoga exercise known as Pore Breathing.

Find yourself a quiet place where you won't be disturbed by people, telephones, pets, etc. If you're sitting down, put your feet together, flat on the floor, hands open loosely on your lap or at your sides. Keep your back fairly straight. If you chose to lie down, don't cross your legs, keep them side by side. Place your arms at your side. They should be comfortable. Gently close your eyes, and do the following steps.

1. <u>Basic Breathing</u> – Basic Relaxation. Focus your attention on your breathing... sense or feel your body breathing in and breathing out. Don't try to change anything, simply be an obser5ver. Do this for two or three minutes. If your Mind drifts away, gently bring it back again and resume mentally watching your breathing. Remember, there's no right way or wrong way in this, so enjoy yourself, and don't hurry anything.

2. <u>Pore Breathing</u> – Now, think or sense your feet... imagine... just imagine you can breathe in and breathe out through your feet. Do this twice. Don't hurry. Next, do it with your legs... imagine the air is coming into your body through the different parts. In your own time, move up through your body – pelvic area, hips, waist, stomach, chest, hands and arms, shoulders, and finally your head. You will notice that by the time you reach your head, your body will be generally

relaxed. Now recognize a deep truth: You did it! You achieved this state of altered consciousness.

When you are relaxed and comfortable, go to the section marked *Sanctuary of the Mind, A Special Place.*

CREATING A SANCTUARY—A SPECIAL PLACE

It helps in beginner's meditation if you have a Special Place, a Sanctuary of the Mind to visit in your meditations. It might be a lovely garden, a secluded sandy beach, a plateau on a mountain top overlooking the world, or a quiet place in a forest. I know one lady who has a Sanctuary in the shape of an ornate Buddhist temple, situated among elegant trees on an island in the middle of a placid lake. Imagine whatever is right for you. Create a Special Place in your mind - image or think about it - and mentally see yourself being there and relaxing. It is important to make your Sanctuary real.

A really good technique for "being there" is when you are in the garden, on the beach, etc, that you occasionally look down and see your feet. This gives you grounding in your Special Place. One other thing: you can create your Sanctuary as big and as detailed as you wish.

Now, it is a good strategy to find a point in your Sanctuary where you can simply relax on a bench, a recliner or a grassy bank where you can simply enjoy the peace and tranquility of Being.

It is in this place that the sub-conscious mind becomes more receptive to change than any other time. You may wish to tell yourself positive affirmations, such as: "Every day in every way, I chose to feel better and better." Mentally repeat this affirmation, slowly, seven times. Then simply relax for a few minutes in your special place.

The Sanctuary may be as large and as spacious as you want. Perhaps a lake, a creek with a rustic bridge, perhaps a healing temple or a temple for prayer. Some people who have trouble exercising, have trails through their Sanctuary and see themselves walking or running.

A Special Place comes in very handy when you wish to have meeting and converse with spirit guides. I have a special alcove among the trees with a white rattan table and chairs, and I meet my guides there.

Another useful facility is an open lawn where you can sit on a bench and say to loved ones in Spirit: "If you are available I would like to meet you." Do this when you feel experienced in True Self consciousness. If you need help in this, I do a meditation on this method of spirit communication on a CD named "Spirit Rendez-vous." prayer

One other thing, know that your Sanctuary of the Mind is your place and it is as private as you wish it to be.

COMING BACK: WIDE AWAKE

When you are ready to return to normal consciousness, take in a slow deep breath, and as you breathe out slowly, say aloud: "Wide awake and eyes open!" And be wide awake. You may also tell yourself: "I am going to count to five, and when I say that number five I will be wide awake and fully alert. One - two - three - four - five."

THE WALKING MEDITATION

Finally, let me leave you with an active meditation as opposed to the stationary techniques above.

Monks in monasteries used to do this, and still do–walk the quadrangle. You can do it too. Find yourself a set path, a circular track or a square, perhaps on a sports field or in a park, a meadow or a large garden. Walk the path and familiarize yourself with the route.

Then, when you are ready to start take in a slow deep breath, then let it out slowly. Be conscious of your body. Feel or sense your entire body. Become totally centered. Then commence your meditative walk with eyes relaxed, watching the ground ahead.

Mentally notice how your body is functioning. Be aware of your feet touching the ground and moving forward. Mentally observe your legs, how your torso is responding, how your arms are moving.

Observe how your head and neck are responding to the walk. Watch how your body feels, particularly if there are any physical changes.

As usual, do not judge or criticize what you are doing, simply be aware of your body. Do not rush this or any other meditation. If a thought comes into your head which says: "This is silly," or "I have to get the dog to the vet," observe them impartially and let them fade away, and continue walking slowly. After 10 or 15 minutes, stop, and get on with your life.

CONCLUSION

Get into the habit of performing a meditation once a day for ten, fifteen or twenty minutes or so and after several days you will notice that you feel more relaxed in your general life, you will have more energy and your sleeping habits may well improve. You will also experience a general sense of well-being.

Enjoy!

AUDIO PROGRAMS THAT MAY HELP YOU

These CD presentations can be found on Robert Egby's website at www.robert-egby.com

CD-107 – Spirit Rendezvous! – Be Your Own Medium! This CD contains three unusual programs – all pertaining to Spirit Communication. (1) A talk on Spirit contact and the Spirit World and instructions for conducting the following meditation. (2) A Meditation for Meeting a Loved One or friends in the Spirit World. (3) The Gatekeeper, a guide who takes you to meet ascended beings or whoever you pray to. Track Two is based on the successful meditation Robert conducted at the first national conference of the American Association of Electronic Voice Phenomena at Reno, Nevada in June 2004.

CD-111 – Discovering the Journey to Loving Yourself. A special self-empowerment program. Throughout the ages the great teachers have told us to "Love Yourself," but legacies have left us with imaginary and pointless limitations. In this program Robert Egby describes the physical, mental and spiritual benefits that come when we let go of limitations and link ourselves to the powerful universal love force – which is our natural heritage. The CD presents a newly recorded beautiful and memorable meditation.

CD-112- The da Vinci Meditation. Leonardo da Vinci the 15th century painter, inventor and philosopher was well aware of higher mystical teachings, particularly the phenomena of Living in the Here and Now. He gave an example in his famous "Notebooks" of how to live in the "Now". Robert has written and recorded a meditation based on this example. The CD presents three tracks: Robert discusses the elements of ancient teachings in "A New Way of Living," followed by "The da Vinci" meditation based on Leonardo's river observations. The CD contains a second meditation: "The Seven Pearls" which highlights the teachings of mystical thinking including living in the Here and Now.

BOOKS AND WEBSITES

I AM by Jean Klein

THE BOOK: ON THE TABOO AGAINST KNOWING WHO YOU ARE by Alan Watts

IN SEARCH OF THE MIRACULOUS by P.D. Ouspensky

THE PHILOSOPHIES AND RELIGIONS OF INDIA by Yogi Rama-charaka

THIS IS YOUR BRAIN ON MUSIC by Daniel J. Levitin

THE WAY OF THE SUFI by Idries Shah

THE LAZY MAN'S GUIDE TO ENLIGHTENMENT by Thaddeus Golas

THE MYSTERY OF CONSCIOUSNESS Article by Steven Pinker, Time – January 19, 2007.

CONFESSIONS by Saint Augustine. Translated: R.S. Pine-Coffin

ZEN O'CLOCK, TIME TO BE by Scott Shaw

THE NOTEBOOKS OF LEONARDO DA VINCI, Edited by Irma A. Richter

THE KING JAMES BIBLE (New Testament for the Sermon on the Mount)

WISDOM OF THE MYSTIC MASTERS by Joseph J. Weed.

HEALING SOUNDS - THE POWER OF HARMONICS by Jonathan Goldman

COSMIC CONSCIOUSNESS: A STUDY OF THE EVOLUTION OF THE HUMAN MIND by Richard Maurice Bucke

SHIFTING FREQUENCIES by Jonathan Goldman

AN ILLUSTRATED ENCYCLOPEDIA OF MYSTICISM by John Ferguson

SOUND HEALING: BIOSONIC REPATTERNING Article by Dr. John Beaulieu www.biosonics.com

THE SLEEP FOUNDATION : Information on sleeping. www.sleepfoundation.org

THE PSYCHIC STREAM by Arthur Findlay

MUSIC AND SOUND IN THE HEALING ARTS by Dr. John Beaulieu

THE EASE OF BEING by Jean Klein

THE FOURTH WAY (The Teachings of Gurdjieff) by P.D. Ouspensky

BOOKS BY ROBERT EGBY

CRACKING THE GLASS DARKLY (Revised and updated 2011)

THE QUEST OF THE RADICAL SPIRITUALIST (2009)

INSIGHTS: THE HEALING PATHS OF THE RADICAL SPIRITUALIST (2010)

KINGS, KILLERS AND KINKS IN THE COSMOS –Treading Softly with Angels Among Minefields. An Autobiography (2011)

All books by Robert Egby are available through Amazon good bookshops throughout the world, Amazon and also at Three Mile Point Publishing, Chaumont, NY.

About the Author

 Robert Egby has helped thousands of people along the path to discover the powers of the True Self. A veteran international journalist, award-winning news photographer and broadcaster, he spent years traveling and observing the human condition. For thirteen years he worked and observed suffering in the Middle East and was an accredited war correspondent at the Suez War.

In 1978 a spirit guide set him on a path to go beyond the study of religion into the realms of higher consciousness and work towards his own True Self, the Cosmic Self. On the way he learned metaphysics, mediumship and healing and taught these in workshops and classes. On the path he discovered a tragedy: millions of people unwittingly live with conditioned, mechanical minds, daily reliving hurtful memories of past events. It was this that encouraged Robert to become an accredited hypnoanalyst and sound healer, professions he practices today. He is also a Spiritualist trained, ordained interfaith minister.

A British medium, Patrick Young once told him: "To achieve your True Self you need to get out of your own way." This book is the result of Robert's search to go beyond the conditioned mind and show that there is a way out for everyone.

CPSIA information can be obtained at www.ICGtesting.com
Printed in the USA
BVOW08s0252210916

462772BV00001B/4/P